THE WILSON LINE OF HULL 1831 TO 1981

The Rise and Fall of an Empire

by

Arthur G. Credland and Michael Thompson

HUTTON PRESS
1994

Published by The Hutton Press Ltd.,
130 Canada Drive, Cherry Burton, Beverley,
East Yorkshire HU17 7SB

Printed and bound by

Clifford Ward (Bridlington) Ltd.,
55 West Street, Bridlington, East Yorkshire, YO15 3DZ

ISBN 1 872167 58 6

CONTENTS

ACKNOWLEDGEMENTS

The writers would like to thank the following for source material: Mr. W. H. Beech, formerly of Ellerman's Wilson Line Ltd. and Mr. Maurice Webster, former archivist to EWL; Mr. Brian Dyson, archivist at the University of Hull; and Jean Sushams, archive assistant; Miss Jill Crowther and the staff of the Hull Local Studies Library; the staff of Hull Technical Library; Mr. Geoffrey Oxley and the staff of the Hull City Record Office; Mr. J. R. Harrower; Wolfgang Kaufmann, Dresden; David Allin, Ships Registry (HM Customs); Mr. Peter Lawson for the preparation of photographic illustrations; and the library staff of Lloyds Register of Shipping. Thanks are also due to Mrs. Anne Lamb who turned a handwritten screed into a readable typescript.

Aerial photographs courtesy Fotoflite, Littlestone Road, New Romney, Kent.

Arthur Credland and
Michael Thompson,
Hull, October 1993

HISTORICAL INTRODUCTION

The Wilson Line, 1831-1981
The Rise and Fall of an Empire

Thomas Wilson was born on 12 February 1792, the son of David and Elizabeth Wilson of Hull. His baptism, two days later, is recorded in the Registers of the Dagger Lane Independent Chapel in which David Wilson is described as a lighterman.[1] The young Thomas was apprenticed in the office of Messrs. Whitaker, Wilkinson and Co. importers of Swedish iron and this promising position as a clerk maybe indicates that his father was now perhaps a lighter *owner* of some substance rather than just employed as a skipper or crewman. It was usual for the parents of an apprentice in a commercial or professional position to pay a premium to the employer for the privilege of obtaining such a post 'with prospects'.

After the completion of his 'time' Thomas was appointed traveller for Sheffield and district and thus became well acquainted with the Yorkshire iron smelters and manufacturers. According to tradition, after his marriage to Susannah West and the rapid growth of his family, he found it necessary to ask his employers for an increase in salary.[2] A refusal led Thomas into the far-reaching decision to set up business on his own. Thirty or so years old he had gained knowledge and experience but was lacking in capital which led him to seek a partner for his new venture and Mr. John Beckinton joined him in the firm of Beckinton, Wilson and Co. iron importers. Initially they were arranging cargoes to be loaded on ships not owned by themselves but eventually began to charter and purchase vessels on their own account. According to tradition Wilson's first vessel was the *Thomas and Ann* but reference to the Hull ship's register indicates that this sloop belonged to a Thomas Wilson, *mariner*, and then only for October to December of 1821. The very first vessel in his possession was the schooner *Swift* which entered the Hull register in 1831 having been transferred from Newcastle. The other shareholders were John Beckinton (of Newcastle), John Hudson, druggist and Thomas Hudson, gentleman, also of Newcastle.[3] Two other vessels were also acquired in 1831, the *Peter and Jane*, schooner, also from Newcastle and the *Oswy*, brigantine, from Whitby. John and Thomas Hudson are described as co-partners in the firm of Beckinton, Wilson and Co. and on 1 December

1836 Beckinton sold his share in all three vessels and the company was reconstituted as Wilson, Hudson & Co. The firm had its office at 14 Salthouse Lane, where Wilson also lived, and it is interesting to note a reminiscence of Benjamin Brooks, son of Thomas Brooks (carver and gilder, Savile Street, Hull). After listing various of the patrons of the family business he says "when a boy, my mother took me in a sedan chair to a ball at Mr. Wilson's home in Salthouse lane". (*Hull News*, Supplement 1897). The address was a convenient one not only because of its nearness to the town docks but it was also next door to the Hull branch of the Bank of England.[4]

Wilson purchased the *Ivanhoe* in 1837, a brig built at Goole, along with John and Thomas Hudson; a John Wilson, possibly a kinsman, was master.[5] On 18 November 1841 Wilson assigned all 64 shares to Thomas Hudson as security for repayment of £2257.12s.6d, with interest, and the power to sell. In the event the executors of the deceased Thomas Hudson re-assigned the shares to Wilson on 9 September 1847 who sold them to his son C. H. Wilson, who in turn sold the vessel the following year.

John and Thomas Hudson had actually withdrawn from the partnership in 1841 and none of the vessels acquired after 1840 included the Hudson's as shareholders. The firm was renamed Thomas Wilson, Sons and Co.. or Thos. Wilson, Sons and Company Ltd. when incorporated in 1891.

The schooner *Patriot* was registered in 1840 as belonging to Thomas' three eldest sons, David, Edward and John but in 1841 sole ownership was vested in their father. One of his Sheffield clients, Charles Cammell, file manufacturer, was part owner of the *Thomas Rickinson* along with Thomas and David Wilson and of the schooner *Dwina*[6] (built at Hull in 1841) along with Thomas Wilson, George Cammell, and Robert Morley Sawyer, master mariner and sometime whaler. Wilson's share in these three vessels was temporarily assigned to Thomas Hudson along with the *Ivanhoe* to secure the loan as related above.

The St. George Steam Packet Co. in 1834 ran the *Superb* and *Cornubia* alternately in a Hull-Gothenburg service which included the carrying of mail. Since no subsidy was forthcoming from the Swedish government they let Beckinton, Wilson and Co. take it over who were already running their sailing vessels to Gothenburg and other Swedish ports. In 1840 when at last support from both Norway and Sweden was forthcoming a regular steam service was established to both countries using the *Glen Albyn* chartered from the Berwick Steam Packet Co. and the *Innisfail* and *St. George* chartered from the St. George Steam Packet Co; the first sailing was 2 June 1840. There were still problems with this service which was discontinued at the end of

Thomas Wilson (1792-1869), founder of the Wilson Line.

David Wilson (1815-93); Thomas' eldest son.

1842 but a settled arrangement was established with the purchase of the *Courier* in 1851 the first steamer to be owned by Wilson's and their only sea-going paddle-driven vessel. Bought from the Leith and Hull Steam Packet Co. she was registered in the names of Thomas and David Wilson until 1853 when the sole ownership was vested in Charles Henry Wilson.[7]

In 1842 Wilson's had considered the Norwegian subsidy inadequate and the route was given up until 1850 when the company received exemption from paying lighthouse and loading fees as payment for carrying mail. From 1852 the route was altered to Hull and Gothenburg via Christiania (Oslo).

Competition in 1856 from the Norwegian company of Det Søndesfjeldske Dampskibsselskab led to a mutual agreement after two years of contention. Then the trade war broke out again in 1866 leading to the demise of the Norwegian firm which had failed to get the support of the countries' leading exporters and importers.

The first steamer purchased as new was the *Scandinavian* built in 1852 by Wingate and Co., Whiteinch, Lanark and the *Baltic* and the *Humber* followed from Alexander Denny of Dunbarton in 1854 in which year the schooner *Patriot* and the brig *Ivanhoe*, the last of the sailing fleet, were sold. In 1857 they were also advertising as agents for the North of Europe Steam Navigation Co. but details of this transaction need to be clarified. 1855 saw the first of many vessels to be built at Earles shipyard at Hull, the *North Sea*, a screw steamer, 209 feet in length. She had only a short career and was lost in 1859 and the *Neva* built at Earles in 1856 was sadly lost the same year, and the *Kingston* also built in 1856 was lost in 1860. The *Atlantic*, fourth vessel from the yard, launched in 1857 was sold to Liverpool owners in 1860. Two names, J. A. and J. E. Wade,[8] timber merchants, figure as principal shareholders of eight of the steamships acquired between 1854 and 1861 but they appear to be sleeping partners with Thomas and David Wilson being the active managers of the company. The Wades involvement ceases in 1859 when they sold their shares in the ss *Atlantic* to David Wilson. There were a number of sales and mortgages of shares within the family e.g. Thomas mortgaged 48 shares of ss *Kingston* to David his son for £3,000, and the same number of shares of the *Atlantic* for £9,000. The latter was redeemed on its sale to Liverpool and subsequently Thomas mortgaged the *Baltic* (Earles 1858) and the *Arctic* (Earles 1859) for £6,000 to David Wilson at 5% interest. Operations were extended by inaugurating the St. Petersburg, Stettin and Riga trades.

In 1847-8 David Wilson had succeeded to the business of his uncle Charles West, wine and spirit merchant, and shortly afterwards took Mr. William (afterwards Alderman) Denison into partnership in the firm of Wilson and Denison. His close involvement with the running of the steamship company ends in 1858 when he relinquishes his partnership but he had minor holdings in various vessels for many years thereafter.[9] The list of Hull shipowners for 1891, two years before his death, credits him as the owner of 5,421 tons.

The Wilson fleet continued to expand, impressively, the *Arctic* (1859), *Bothnia* (1860), *Argo* (1860), *Pacific* (1860), *Albion* (1861), *Oder* (1861), *Juno* (1861), *Hebe* (1861), *Hero* (1861), *Trent* (1862), *Ouse* (1862), *Dido* (1862), *North Eastern* (1863), *United Service* (1864), *Clio* (1864), *Juno* (1864), *Sappho* (1864), *Apollo* (1865), *Milo* (1865), *Calypso* (1865), *Bravo* (1866), *Baron Hambro* (1866), *Echo* (1866) *Hero* (1866), *Cato* (1867), *Otto* (1867), *Fido* (1868), *Gozo* (1868), *Plato* (1868), *Nero* (1868) and *Ino* (1868).

On 21 June 1869 Thomas Wilson passed away at his home, Park House, Cottingham, leaving a wonderful legacy for his two sons to build on.[10] In fact it is clear from the pattern of share-holdings that he had pulled out of active involvement several years before his death. In 1861 he disposed of his interest in most of the fleet to his two sons Charles Henry and Arthur Wilson and thereafter new tonnage is in their name, occasionally with David as a minor shareholder and other outside parties.[11] The ss *Milo*, built at Glasgow 1865, was initially registered in sole ownership of Arthur Wilson but subsequently 8 shares (each) were sold to John Loft, gentleman, R. C. Cook, merchant, James Dossor, surgeon, and David Wilson. From 1866 new vessels built were jointly in the hands of Charles and Arthur, sometimes with the participation of David, and mortgages frequently were taken out with their father e.g. *Hero* (1866) mortgaged for £13,000 at 5%, *Cato* (1867) for £12,000 at 5%. All the surviving vessels were eventually acquired in 1891 by the private limited company of Thomas Wilson, Sons and Co.

During the Franco-Prussian war the various Prussian ports were closed causing the suspension of the Stettin trade. This circumstance was turned to advantage by developing a new route to Trieste which developed into a regular Adriatic trade later expanded to Sicily. After the cessation of hostilities in France the Stettin service was resumed and a Danzig trade was also begun. More steamers had been sent to Western Norway in 1867 after achieving domination on the Christiania route resulting from the collapse of Det Søndenfjeldske. This expansion encouraged by the export of pyrites from the mines at Ytterøya, Sunnhardland and Karmøy. Calling at Bergen and Stavanger the Hull ships carried a variety of England goods outwards including fine textiles. A dramatic expansion of the company's horizons come with the establishing of an Indian route from London through the Suez canal, which had opened for business in 1869, the year Thomas Wilson had died. Larger vessels of some 2500-3000 tons were planned for the new service but the *Orlando* (bt. Earles 1870) originally in the Gothenburg trade was the first steamer to arrive at Hull direct from India.

She had sailed on her outward voyage to Bombay via London in August 1871 and in December the same year, the ss *Thomas Wilson* began the Calcutta service, followed by the *Virago* and *Zeno*. The *Colombo*, *Hindoo* and *Othello* were all launched in 1872, *Colombo* at Humphrys and Pearsons yard in Hull and *Othello* at Earles but *Hindoo* at Lawries, a Glasgow yard. Two more vessels from Earles yard, *Eldorado* and *Navarino* joined the fleet trading to Colombo, Madras and Calcutta.

A great many of the Wilson vessels of this period, particularly those built at Earles, were recorded in the ship portraits of Samuel Henry Wilson, possibly a kinsman of the shipowners. He painted only in watercolours and gouache and for an oil painting of the *Hindoo*, Samuel Walters, the notable Liverpool marine artist, was chosen. Reproduced in the *Illustrated London News* of 1872 it was accompanied by the following description:

> "The Saloon, which is 54ft long by 22ft wide, is on the upper deck, amidship, and is constructed with an overhanging deck on each side of the saloon, for the protection of the passengers in hot climates, while it also affords protection from rain, the passengers at the same time being able to take open air exercise. The comfort of the passengers has been considered in every respect, the ship being thoroughly ventilated, with large square ports, and furnished with baths, hot and cold, and with electric bells, close to the berths in every state-room. Beside the upper saloon, there are two separate sitting saloons for ladies; and two smoking-rooms, on deck, for gentlemen. The fine after-saloon, and spacious cabins afford comfortable accommodation for forty second-class passengers, with ladies' cabins and bath-rooms also. The ship is barque-rigged with iron masts.
>
> The owners of the *Hindoo* have just got another large steamer completed, the *Colombo* of 2800 register, and similar to the vessel we have described."[12]

The firm was now firmly on the world stage and in 1875 Wilson's were confident enough to venture into the North American trade up till then dominated by the well-established Liverpool shipping companies. They had studied the American markets in grain and produce very carefully and set about buying their own cargoes as well as supplying the goods in their own vessels and thereby took a threefold profit as merchants, brokers and shippers. The reluctant American brokers soon came into line to deal with this new 'upstart' company and by the end of the century the American trade was the largest and most successful branch of Wilson's truly international trade.

The *Othello* was transferred from India and the *Colombo*, *Otranto*, *Lepanto*, *Rialto*, *Marengo* and *Salerno* joined the Atlantic fleet. Excessive competition on the Indian routes led to its discontinuation soon after pioneering the New York service but in 1883 a Hull and Bombay line was established utilising the *Othello* which was taken from the Atlantic fleet. This vessel and many of the vessels in the U.S. trade were captured on canvas by the notable marine painter Antonio Jacobsen of New York. From 1879 the New York agents were Sanderson and Son and Oswald Sanderson[13] was to play a key role in Wilson company affairs until well after the 1916 take over. In the 1890s Wilson steamers were carrying more cargo to and from New York than the vessels of any other firm, with passages from Hull, the Tyne and London as well as from Gothenburg, Stettin and Copenhagen. They also ran a line of steamers from Antwerp to Boston and Baltimore. In 1893 no less than 18 vessels were employed in the New York service alone, with a combined tonnage of 57,000 tons (dead weight) capable of carrying 75,000 tons of cargo and averaging seven voyages per vessel each year, which combined to make a total of nearly one million tons of cargo. An element in the success of the trade was the high quality steamships built at Earles shipyard with their advanced compound and triple expansion engines.

The *Martello* (Earles, 1884) was probably the first *newly-built* steamer with triple expansion engines to be put on the N. Atlantic run.

In 1887 (possibly even as early as 1885) joint advertisements were made under the title of Wilson and Furness Lines operating to New York from Newcastle via Dundee and in 1896 a joint company the Wilson and Furness Leyland Line was launched.

For use in the N. American trade sailing from London three vessels were purchased (apparently in 1887 but not registered in Hull until 1893), from the Royal Exchange Shipping Co. of London, named the *Egyptian Monarch*, *Lydian Monarch* and *Persian Monarch*. The latter was sold in 1894 to a New York owner and gains a small niche in history by being the vessel used to transport back to the USA Buffalo Bill's 'Wild West show' after a successful tour of the UK.

Old established business interests were not however being neglected and in 1874 the splendid new vessel *Angelo* was

*The schooners **Dwina** and **Ellen Crawford**; an oil painting by John Ward of Hull.*

launched by Humphrys and Pearson of Hull for the Gothenburg service. 1547 tons gross, 258 feet in length this vessel attracted the attention of the London press and a lengthy description appeared in the *Illustrated London News* in August 1874.

"The steamers from Hull to Christiania and Gothenburg belonging to Messrs. Thomas Wilson, Sons and Company of Hull are vessels of a very superior class. The *Angelo* lately placed under the command of Capt. Nicholson, is a fine vessel, handsomely and conveniently fitted up. She was built by Messrs. Humphrys and Pearson (limited liability company). Her dimensions are as follows: length 262ft; breadth of beam 33ft 6in; depth of hold 18ft; tonnage 1,600. She has been built under special survey, and is classed 20 years in the Liverpool register. Her lines are very fine. The accommodation for passengers is superior to that of most vessels afloat. The dining room is entirely separate from the dormitories and there is a magnificent drawing-room apart from the staterooms or the dining saloon.

The vessel is pooped for fully three parts of her entire length, and there is a top gallant forecastle 35ft long. The bulwarks between the forecastle and the poop are about 7ft high. At the aft end is a teak-built deckhouse which is a smoking room, reading room or lounge, for the use of passengers. The house is fitted up in mahogany and upholstered in green leather.

Next comes a huge iron galley with ventilating roof. The galley is divided by a partition. One side is for the cooking for first class passengers, the other for emigrants who are brought to Hull on their way to America.

Amidships is a substantial teak-built house, which rests upon iron coamings. This is the dining saloon 43ft long and 15ft wide. The roof of the dining-room is a promenade for the first class passengers; all round it are seats for their accommodation. The saloon within is a luxuriously fitted apartment. The cabinet work is of polished mahogany, and the sofas and settees are upholstered in crimson velvet. The floor is covered with a rich oilcloth, on which handsome Brussels carpet-runners are laid. The sides of the saloon are panelled in maple, with wainscot frames and rosewood mouldings. In the centre of each frame an ebony pilaster springs from the top of the sofa.

These pilasters terminate in richly carved and gilded capitals, and support a cornice in white and gold. At the after end of the saloon is a pantry. The drawing room may be entered from either side of the vessel. This room is 18ft wide and occupies the forepart of the poop. It is not less magnificently fitted. The style of the woodwork is in keeping with that of the dining saloon but the upholstery is green velvet, which offers a fine contrast of colour with the gilded carved work. The sofas are fixed across each end and the front side of the place reserved for a Broadwood piano. The floor is covered with a velvet pile carpet, of rich pink and blue pattern. Altogether the drawing room is most elegant and affords a degree of comfort and convenience rarely attained on board ship. The staterooms most of which are double berth afford accommodation to 74 passengers. There is a saloon for the exclusive use of lady passengers, and connecting with the stewardesses berth.

Outwardly as well as inwardly the *Angelo* presents a handsome appearance. She is rigged with three pole masts, and with fore and aft canvas. The fore and main masts are iron and the mizzenmast of wood. The whole of the standing rigging is of wire rope. The sails consist of fore, main and mizzen topsails, stay foresail and jib and mizzen staysails. For the shipping and discharging of cargo three stern winches have been provided. The anchor is weighed by Harfields patent steam windlass which works with its own engine by steam supplied from the main boilers. The *Angelo* is propelled by a pair of compound surface condensing engines of 300 horse power, nominal, each are expected to develop 1400 indicated horse power. The high pressure cylinder is 41in in diameter, and the low pressure 72in with a 42in stroke. The engines are driven with two double-ended boilers, carrying a working pressure of 80lb to the square inch. The vessel can attain a speed of 12 knots."

In 1878 Wilson's purchased the fleet of Brownlow, Marsdin a company descended from the Hull Steam Packet Co., pioneers of steam shipping on the Humber. The firm originally incorporated a shipbuilding and engineering capacity and the latter function was embraced by C. D. Holmes, a Hull engineering firm which continued in business as makers of engines and winches until the collapse of the Hull fishing industry in 1975.[14] A lack of orders for new trawlers and the concomitant fittings forced them into liquidation.

Seven vessels were acquired: the *Falcon, Leopard, Lumsden, Marsdin, Panther, Tiger* and *Zebra*, four of these vessels had been built by Brownlow and Pearson and another by Humphrys and Pearson. They were regulars in the Hamburg, Antwerp and Dunkirk trade and continued in service with Wilson though only three of the vessels were actually given new names with the Wilson 'O' ending. The *Argo* in 1860 was the first ship with what became a typical Wilson name but the practise was not established

Charles Henry Wilson (1833-1907), later Lord Nunburnholme of Warter Priory.

Arthur Wilson (1836-1906) of Tranby Croft, Master of the Holderness Hunt.

as a rule for all vessels built to the order of the company until *Clio* in 1864. Thereafter only chartered vessels or ships brought from other owners had a different style of name.

Wilson's domination of the Norwegian trade began to slacken when in 1880 Ostlandske Lloyd opened a fortnightly run between Larvik and Newcastle. Initially their business was based on wood pulp but later passengers became more important until in 1906 they were taken over by Fred Olsen.

Emigrants were a significant part of Wilson's business at this time when many thousands of Swedes and Norwegians were leaving for the new world escaping the severely depressed economy at home.[15] There was also a surge of Jewish refugees displaced during the Tsarist pogroms in the Baltic States. P. G. Halvorsen tried to break the Wilson monopoly with a service from Bergen to Newcastle and in 1886 applied for a state subsidy in order to secure the survival of his line. At the end of the decade this venture led to the formation of the Norwegian England line.

By an 1889 act of parliament the Manchester, Sheffield and Lincolnshire Railway Co. gained sailing privileges into a number of Norwegian ports and so as to avoid competition Wilson's reached an agreement with them whereby Wilson vessels sailing to Gothenburg and east Norway terminated at Grimsby. In 1892 Wilson's began a Grimsby-Gothenburg service to which the M. S. and L. were forced to acquiesce in order to avoid a damaging freight war.

In response to both the establishment of the Norwegian England line in 1890 and the increasing number of small direct sailing vessels in the fresh herring trade Wilson's freight rates were dramatically lowered between Trondheim and Hull, and had already been decreased by 40% for the Oslo-Hull route even before this. Another reaction to the Norwegian England line was the introduction of a new Bergen-Hamburg route but by 1891 Wilson's came to an accommodation with Det Bergenske, Det Nordenfjeldske and Halvorsen, and ceased this traffic in exchange for the regulation of freight charges on the West Norway — England lines. By such means Wilson's continued to dominate the Norwegian trade until the First World War a position which came under considerable pressure from the Swithun Line formed in 1910 to satisfy the interests of canning and tin factories in Bergen, Haugesund, Kopervik and Stavanger. The success of the new venture also seriously affected the Det Bergenske and Det Nordenfjeldske Steamship Companies and the freight war eventually resulted in arbitration involving all the interested parties who agreed on a common rate.

In 1887 the Wilson Line seems to have carried most of the fresh herring which came into London and Hull and at the latter provided the raw materials for the biggest concentration of kipper houses in Britain. By the early 1890s however, fast steamships sailing direct from the fishing grounds and built especially for the trade had taken the lion's share. The freight rates were only slightly lower on these vessels but the improved quality due to careful handling and a more rapid service resulted in increased profits of up to two shillings a box greater than that sent with the regular liners. White fish, especially halibut, were also imported by Wilson vessels sailing to Hull from Trondheim via Kristiansund N. and Aalesund and also via Bergen if required.

Another route was from Bergen to Hull via Stavanger and a determined attempt was made to link with the regular fish landings but the Norwegian skippers were not always co-operative and considerable losses were suffered by Wilson's in this trade.

The legal status of the firm altered when in January 1891 it became a private limited company, Thomas Wilson Sons and Co. Ltd., with a share capital of £2 million made up of 20,000, £100 units. Charles Henry Wilson was Chairman and Arthur Wilson the other principal though David Wilson was at least nominally a director too. Three years later they purchased the Hull — Newcastle coasting trade maintaining a regular weekly service.

Many of the fine new steamers of the Wilson fleet had been built by C. and W. Earle reformed as Earles Shipbuilding and Engineering Co. after the death of W. J. Earle in 1871. At the end of the nineteenth century persistent labour problems, which meant that the engineering department was paralysed for 53 weeks in a three year period, resulted in a chronic lack of capital. In June 1900 the directors put the company into voluntary liquidation and were immensely grateful when in the following year Charles Henry Wilson purchased the yard for £150,000 and injected £170,000 of new capital to restart operations.[16] The new firm retained the same name as its predecessor and was a private limited company. Almost half the output in the years leading up to the First World War was for the Wilson Line and because of this the shipyard was cushioned from the worst effects of the lean years of 1906-8.

The acquisitions of the Wilson Line reached a climax in 1903 with the purchase of the Bailey and Leetham fleet. At the time the latter was second only to Wilson's among the steamship companies operating out of Hull. They were heavily committed to the Baltic trade with services to St. Petersburg, Konigsberg, Copenhagen, Reval as well as Hamburg and (from London) ran to Venice, Trieste and Palermo. At one stroke Wilson's had eliminated a major rival and obtained the extra tonnage to boost their trade with northern Europe and the Mediterranean.

The merger as the move was termed, but in reality a takeover by Wilson's, was essential to both parties. B. and L. relied heavily on the Baltic Trade and both companies were under pressure from the expanding activities of the Det Forenede Dampskibs Selskab (DFDS), founded at Copenhagen in 1866. The intense competition had seriously lowered the freight rates and William S. Bailey negotiated the sale of his company, which, including all the fleet and real estate, he valued at £650,000. Charles Henry Wilson offered £350,000 and the deal was settled on 15 July 1903. The issue of the *Shipping World and Herald of Commerce*, dated 29 July 1903 carried the following report misleadingly referring to an *amalgamation*:

"On the 20 inst. it was announced that Thomas Wilson and Sons Ltd. the well-known Hull firm, had effected an amalgamation with Messrs. Bailey and Leetham, another large firm of shipowners in Hull. Both these firms have for many years been keen rivals in the Baltic trade and, whereas a healthy competition is always good for the trade, there is no doubt that it had become too keen and an amalgamation of the rivals be desirable. The new concern will be among the largest in the country, having a capital of £2,500,000. Messrs. Wilson contribute £2,000,000 and the balance is found by Messrs. Bailey and Leetham. The business will be carried out just as before and there will be no change in the fleets or personnel of the respective staffs."

One of the masters who came to Wilson's after this deal was William Barron, sometime master of the *Kaffraria*, who had spent his formative years in the Hull whaling trade and in 1861 commanded the famous old *Truelove*[17] which had made an amazing 72 voyages to the Arctic fishery.

Twenty-three vessels were acquired most of which did excellent service in the years before the outbreak of war, although seven of them were sold on to other companies from 1904 to 1906. All those which were retained kept their original names but were repainted in the Wilson livery.

From this position of strength Oswald Sanderson, now a director of Wilson's, was able to work out an agreement with DFDS. Wilson's and DFDS were to run vessels between Hull and Copenhagen and Newcastle and Copenhagen with an equal number of sailings, the gross earnings to be pooled. The Hull-Konigsberg and Hull-Windau services were also shared but the Hull-Libau route was to be exclusive to the Danish company. There were also to be equal sailings on the London, Copenhagen, Konigsberg route and the two firms were to be exclusive agents one for the other. Wilson's were also to be agents for DFDS for the purchase of coal supplied from the Humber ports. The link between DFDS and Wilson's persisted until the disposal of the last of the Wilson fleet in 1981 and in both World Wars Wilson's managed DFDS vessels seized by the British authorities.

In March 1904 Wilson had a total of 99 vessels and four tugs and they could provide an improved service of first class vessels from London to St. Petersburg, Reval, Riga and Copenhagen as well as from Hull.

A joint London office, under the title of United Shipping Co. Ltd. was established to undertake the DFDS agency as well as general shipping and insurance business.

Wilson's established branch offices at all the chief commercial and industrial centres, at Manchester, Leeds, Sheffield and Birmingham as well as Grimsby from where steamers also ran regularly to Gothenburg, Malmo, Christiania (Oslo) and the Baltic ports, which destinations were also served from Manchester and Liverpool. To enhance the home trades and ensure the full co-operation of the railways in linking with their services Wilson established in 1906 a joint enterprise with the North Eastern Railway Co. Entitled the Wilson's and North Eastern Railway Shipping Co. Ltd. it operated between Hamburg, Antwerp, Ghent, Dunkirk and Hull.[18] The fleet comprised the *Juno*, *Bruno*, *Otto*, *Cito*, *Truro*, *Dynamo* and *Hero*. Wilsons had always prided themselves on being self-sufficient, to the extent of having their own printing works which produced most of the company's bills of lading, brochures, handbills, captains' manuals and the abundance of forms required by a world-wide shipping enterprise.

Long before the purchase of Earles shipyard, Arthur Wilson had in 1874 formed a partnership with Charles Frederick Amos and his brother-in-law Henry Wilson Ringrose Smith to found the Amos and Smith engineering company. Both the Ringroses and the Voases to whom he was connected, were important Hull merchants and shipowners. For many years they were the local rivals of C. D. Holmes in the building of steam engines and ships' fittings and most Hull trawlers were equipped by one or other of these two firms. When Smith died in 1890 his interest was purchased by C. H. Wilson.[19]

Charles Henry Wilson, Liberal member of parliament for Hull had been the active promoter of the expansion of the company's activities throughout the globe. As the biggest privately owned shipping company in the world it played a major role in maintaining Hull's place as the nation's third largest port and was crucial to the employment prospects, directly or indirectly, of thousands of Hull's citizens. In 1906 Charles Wilson was rewarded by being ennobled as Lord Nunburnholme but sadly

*The SS **Hindoo**, 1872; an oil painting by Samuel Walters of Liverpool.*

Captain with officers and smart young stewardesses aboard an unidentified Wilson Steamer c.1900.

did not live long to enjoy his new status and died on 27 October 1907.[20] A staunch liberal and though an opponent of the Boer War his patriotism was never in doubt and he gave the use of the ss *Ariosto* and *Toronto* without charge to the government for transport of the City (of London) Imperial Volunteers to Cape Town, in 1900.

His interests extended to the local trawling industry and Wilson was Vice-chairman of the Hull Steam Fishing and Ice Co. (Red Cross Box Fleet). After the infamous attack on the Hull fishing fleet on the Dogger Bank (21 October 1904) by the Russian navy he was invited to unveil the memorial to the dead at the corner of the Boulevard, Hessle Road. Owing however to his indisposition the monument was unveiled on 30 August 1906 by John Watt J.P.

Wilson Line masters were no strangers to dramatic rescues 'on the high seas' but in 1908 one was able to make a contribution on shore. The ss *Ebro* was tied up at the port of Messina, Sicily, on 26 December when there was a devastating earthquake in Calabria at the toe of Italy. The resulting tidal wave lifted her virtually onto the quayside and all her plates on one side were damaged before settling back into the sea. As soon as the initial shock had subsided Capt. Duffill organised his crew into shore parties who managed to bring out of the ruins members of the British community living there. The sixteen adults and three babies saved were taken to Palermo and to acknowledge the efforts of the master and crew the King of Italy awarded a medal to each man. Capt. Duffill and the chief mate were made chevaliers and were given a white cross set with a ruby, the remainder each received a cross suspended on a white and green ribbon. The vessel itself was sold four years later to Greek owners and was torpedoed in 1917.

From the family's humble beginnings the two generations had built the Wilson company into a shipping phenomenon. Thomas had established a comfortable if not especially grand house in Cottingham but increasing wealth led his sons to a more opulent display.

Charles Henry Wilson purchased and improved the seventeenth century Warter Priory and took his title from the neighbouring village.[21] Arthur Wilson chose to build anew and purchased 34 acres of land at Tranby Croft, near Anlaby on the western outskirts of Hull. The foundation stone was laid by his son Arthur Stanley and the family eventually moved into their splendid house with its sixty rooms and three storeys, in the late summer of 1876. Here Arthur Wilson was able to entertain friends, colleagues and fellow members of the Holderness Hunt. An enthusiastic fox-hunting man, he was most commonly photographed dressed for the field. In 1878 he agreed to become

Master and he generously supported the Holderness to the tune of some £4,000 a year until he retired as MFH in 1903. His wealth and position in society also gained him an association with the Prince of Wales and his set who in September 1890 were persuaded to stay at Tranby Croft during the St. Leger race meeting at Doncaster. This culminated in the 'Baccarat Scandal' when Col. Sir William Gordon Cumming was accused of cheating at cards. A libel case brought by Col. Cumming resulted in the Prince of Wales being called as a witness and providing the newspapers and the public with the spectacle of the heir to the throne openly admitting his active involvement in what was then an illegal gambling game. The Wilson family seem to have come through the ordeal relatively unscathed and Muriel Wilson, Arthur's daughter, was to make a considerable impression on fashionable society, and at one time the wealthy heiress was pursued by the young Winston Churchill as a possible wife.

Arthur Wilson who became chairman of the company following the death of his brother Lord Nunburnholme, died on 21 October, 1909 aged 71.[22] Kenneth Wilson, one of his sons became chairman in his stead firmly establishing the third generation of family control of this great shipping line. Lord Nunburnholme (Charles Henry Wilson's son) was appointed deputy chairman, Mr. Oswald Sanderson, managing director and Clive Wilson and the Hon. Guy Wilson MP (sons of Arthur and Charles respectively) were also on the board.

The outbreak of war in 1914 had a disastrous effect on the company and throughout the hostilities nearly fifty ships were lost to enemy action. Several of the old Bailey and Leetham vessels were sold to the Admiralty for use as blockships to protect the naval anchorage at Scapa Flow from enemy attack. Other vessels were held by the Germans, having been caught in German ports at the outbreak of hostilities and although some of their men were subsequently repatriated the rest spent the war in internment camps, notably Ruhleben on the outskirts of Berlin.[23] The splendid twin-funnel RMS *Eskimo* a magnificent steel vessel of 3326 tons built at Earles in 1910 was initially converted into a merchant cruiser but found to be unsuitable she was disarmed and put back into the Hull-Norway trade. Captured in 1916 she was used as a net-layer (presumably for ship and harbour defence) by the Germans.

Once a favourite for summer cruises to Norway she was returned after the war ended but was never restored to her former elegance and was sold to France in 1921. The *Aaro* built in 1909, also at Earles, and the first ship on the Humber to carry wireless, was torpedoed in September 1916 with the loss of three crew; the remainder were taken into captivity. Yet another Earles-built vessel the *Castro* (1911) was one of the vessels in Germany when war was declared. Lying in the Kiel Canal she was to find a place in the convoluted story of Irish nationalism. At the instigation of Sir Roger Casement she was used in an attempt to supply arms to the Irish insurgents. First named *Libau* she was then disguised as the Norwegian cargo vessel *Aud*, ostensibly a merchant vessel with its pit props and general cargo. She successfully penetrated the English blockade without being identified but the reception party that was supposed to meet her in Tralee Bay on 20 April 1916 failed to appear. Her captain then turned for home but the armed trawler *Lord Heneage* became suspicious and gave chase though she was too slow to close with the gun runner. Then two naval sloops appeared on the scene and Captain Karl Spindler scuttled his ship and surrendered to the navy.[24] Two other Wilson vessels the *Borodino* and *Gourko* had careers serving the British forces stationed in Orkney. The *Borodino* like *Castro* built at Earles in 1911 was chartered by the Junior Army and Navy Stores as an officers' supply ship anchored at Scapa Flow for the convenience of the Grand Fleet. Designated MFA No.6, boxing competitions, theatrical performances, concerts and billiards matches were held on board while at the same time she functioned as a floating multiple store with departments to satisfy all needs.[25] *Borodino* also made a contribution in the Second World War when in 1940 she was sunk as a block ship at Zeebrugge.

The *Gourko* also built at Earles in 1911 was used as a supply vessel to the Orkney forces but in between shipments of meat a stage and auditorium were set up as required for live performances and film shows. The officers and men of the Grand Fleet subsequently presented a silver shield to the *Gourko* which under the command of Captain J. R. Owen had been the venue for seven hundred entertainments witnessed by over three hundred thousand officers and men. Returned to Wilson's in 1919 she also ended her life as a block ship, this time at Dunkirk, in June 1940.

The impact of the Great War was such that the Wilson family had seriously to consider their position. Such was the loss of tonnage and more importantly the advance of their neutral rivals while their own activities had been so drastically curtailed, that it was decided to sell the company. The events in Russia and the rumblings of revolution with their unpredictable effects on the Baltic trade were possibly also taken into consideration. The result was the unthinkable and a dramatic public announcement, which shocked the people of Hull, that the great shipping company so identified with the city had been sold to Sir John Reeves Ellerman Bt. It is interesting to note that he himself had been born at Hull (100 Anlaby Road) in 1862 the son of a Hamburg merchant, of Danish origin, though had left here while still a young boy.[26] In 1915 Ellerman Lines Ltd. of Liverpool had a fleet of 97 vessels with a gross tonnage of 462,000 tons and Ellerman and Bucknall Steamship Co. Ltd. (Liverpool) had a further 29 ships, aggregating 14,000 tons. Ellermans ranked as the eighth largest steamship firm in the world and Wilson as the twenty-eighth. Ellerman Lines includced City Line, Bucknall Line, Hall Line and the Papayanni Line and Sir John had interests embracing brewing in both Britain and America.[27]

In January 1917 the name was changed to Ellerman's Wilson Line Ltd. but the vessels retained their distinctive livery of a green hull and a red funnel with a black top. The Ellerman house flag, a blue burgee with the letters J. R. E. was flown above a swallow tailed pennant, white with a red ball, the original Wilson house flag; popularly regarded as representing the last drop of blood that could be squeezed out of the staff! Sir John Ellerman became chairman of the new company with Oswald Sanderson as managing director; E. Kenneth Wilson[28], Edward Lloyd and Capt. J. R. Westcott were directors.

Post war was a time of a reconstruction and rebuilding with new vessels ordered to replace numerous gaps in the fleet. *Grodno*, *Polo*, *Thurso*, *Trentino* and *Urbino* were all launched in 1919, in various yards, Dundee, Sunderland, and W. Hartlepool; only *Urbino* was built in Hull, at Earles. The latter yard did however produce vessels for the Ellerman 'empire' the *City of Durban* and *City of Christiania* in 1921 and the *City of HongKong*, 1924 but thereafter very few Ellerman vessels were ordered there. There was the *Salerno* (1924) and *Teano* (1925), the *City of Worcester* in 1927 and no more before the yard's closure in 1931 at the time of the Depression. Ships were moved about between the Ellerman companies, *Destro* and *Dido* went to Liverpool in 1925 and *Rollo* was transferred from Ellerman City Line in 1920. A series of vessels, *Calypso*, *Carlo*, *Cato*, *Leo*, *Manchuria*, *Torcello*, *Vasco*, *Iago*, were bought from the Shipping Controller in 1920 having been acquired as war prizes or reparations.

In 1926 Engvald Baldersheim of Bergen, Norway, began an enterprise off Greenland in which halibut caught by line from a flotilla of dories were packed in the refrigerated hold of a mother ship. The first of these was the *Helder* which brought its fish into Hull by arrangements with Hellyers Steam Fishing Co. partners with the Norwegian in this undertaking.[29]

Helder and another vessel the *Vasari* were respectively renamed the *Arctic Prince* and *Arctic Queen* in 1928 after being put in the British register to avoid a 10% tax on foreign caught fish. The Wilson vessel *Borodino* took supplies to these vessels and

*The SS **Angelo**, 1874.*

then returned to Hull with the fish and the *Mourino* also made two trips to Davis Strait for the same purpose. Capt. Ashford of the *Borodino* also took with him to Upernavik in 1928 a film unit, plus aeroplane and pilot from Hamburg. A polar bear was essential to the film's storyline and in order not to waste time hunting for a wild bear, which probably would not have been manageable anyway, an animal was actually taken all the way to Greenland from Hagenbach Zoo in Germany! The beast eventually escaped and the pilot Ernst Udet, the wartime fighter ace went in search for the missing polar exploration airship *Italia* commanded by Umberto Nobile. 1935 saw the formation of Associated Humber Lines a grouping of the vessels of Goole Steam Shipping Co. (L. M. S. Railway) and the two Hull based companies the Hull and Netherlands Steamship Co. and Wilson's and North Eastern Railway Shipping Co. along with the LNER Continental Services at Grimsby.

However war clouds were gathering yet again and Ellerman's Wilson Line was to suffer its share of the terrible toll on merchant shipping as a result of the determined German blockade of Britain and the U-boat campaign which threatened to strangle our lifeline of food and raw materials.

The *Bury, Accrington, Dewsbury, Stockport,* and *Melrose Abbey* of the AHL fleet were used as rescue ships for the Atlantic convoys.[30] *Mourino* (1906) and *Carlo* (1911) were sold to the Admiralty as ammunition hulks; the *Salerno* was captured by the Germans during the Norwegian campaign and used as a torpedo recovery vessel in the Baltic, renamed *Markirch*; and the *Salmo* was captured by the Vichy French at Casablanca, also in 1940, and scuttled two years later. The *Salerno* was actually retaken in 1945 and after returning to the Wilson fleet in 1946, as the *Empire Salerno* (of London) and later *Salerno* once more, remaining on the London register she remained in service for another ten years.

At least some of the Wilson officers and crew had an opportunity to take the battle to the enemy when in 1943 they were recruited by the SOE (Special Operations Executive) to bring supplies of much needed ball-bearings and specialist metals from neutral Sweden.

Five 117ft motor gun boats were prepared to run the German blockade, the most dangerous part of the journey being the narrows of the Skaggerak where they were exposed to German fast patrol boats, coastal guns and aircraft. Each vessel *Nonsuch* (Cap. H. Jackson) *Hopewell* (Capt. David Stokes), *Gay Viking* (Capt. Henry Whitfield), *Gay Corsair* (Capt. Robert Tanton) and *Master Standfast* (Capt. George Holdsworth) was armed with two twin oerlikons, two twin Vickers and a Quadruple Vickers but

essentially relied on its speed to evade attack and get to and from Lysekil in Sweden as quickly as possible. Operation Bridford was a great success and after leaving Immingham on the Humber on 26 October *Gay Viking* was back at Immingham on the 31st with a precious cargo of 40 tons of ball-bearings. *Master Standfast* was badly mauled by a German patrol vessel and Captain Holdsworth, who later died of his wounds, and his crew were captured.[31] Seven trips were made between October 1943 and March 1944.

At the beginning of hostilities the Ellerman Wilson fleet had numbered 35 ships whereas by the end of the war this had been reduced to single figures a mere nine! A major rebuilding programme was instigated by H. S. Holden, chairman of Wilson's since 1933 and of Ellerman Lines from 1944, until his death in 1946. By this time 9 vessels had been built and Mr. J. W. Bayley,[32] who succeeded him as chairman of the Wilson Line, and subsequently of Ellerman Lines, pursued the building policy with such energy and enterprise that from 1947 to the time of his death in December 1950, 12 more vessels had been completed followed by the addition of 2 more in 1951-2. Mr. J. R. Fewlass followed Mr. Bayley as chairman of the company, a position he held until his death in 1959.[33]

He was the last chairman of Ellerman's Wilson Line Ltd. before it became a wholly owned subsidiary of Ellerman Lines, London. Sir John Ellerman, having continued to hold Wilson's directly and distinct from his other shipping interests, which were all controlled through Ellerman Lines Ltd. This special status for the Hull firm is probably an indication of his special affection for the city where he had been born.

One of the long-lasting after-effects of the war were the allied forces garrisoned in large numbers on German soil. In 1945 the Ministry of War transport had placed the management of the *Empire Wansbeck* (an ex-German vessel) with Wilson's. On the Harwich-Hook of Holland service she made 2,030 voyages carrying a total of 1,821,324 service personnel until the movement of men was replaced by air transport in 1961.

Post-war reconstruction and a new spirit of optimism reached a climax with the coronation of Queen Elizabeth in 1953. A part of the celebrations was to take place at Spithead in a review of the naval and merchant fleets, on the 15 June. Wilson's sent their representative the ss *Borodino* built at Troon in 1950 for the Hull-Copenhagen service and she arrived on the Solent spick and span under the command of Captain Ford. He had joined the company in 1911 following in his father's footsteps, and was a younger brother of Hull Trinity House. Accompanying *Borodino* were two other Hull vessels the

Wilson staff had an active social life, cricket, football, hockey, angling being among the most popular. In 1906 their band won the Peoples Challenge Shield at Crystal Palace.

*The SS **Ebro** whose crew were heroes of the 1908 Italian earthquake.*

trawler *Loch Torridon*, pioneer of the all year round Greenland fishery, and the *Magrix*.

One of the first of the new launchings after the war, the *Bravo*, built by Henry Robb of Leith in 1947, featured in the film 'Berth 24'. Produced for BTC (British Transport Commission) this survives as an important documentary record of a typical round trip between Hull and Gothenburg, capturing the details of loading and unloading by the Hull dockworkers before containerisation took over from traditional methods.

AHL also needed new vessels to replace war losses and some of the more elderly units. Two new refrigerated cargo vessels, the *Kirkham Abbey* and the *Byland Abbey*[34] were managed for the British Transport Commission in the Goole-Copenhagen service and British Railways ferry services on the Humber (Hull to New Holland) also came under AHL management. In order to rationalise the German service, Goole-Hamburg and Hull-Bremen-Hamburg, an association was formed with Argo Line of Bremen whose vessels *Arcturus* and *Antares* were regulars on these routes. 1957 saw AHL floated as a limited company with a £3.5 million share capital, 91% held by BTC and 9% by EWL, the chairman was Herbert Arthur Short, with G. W. Bayley, S. J. Bird, Arthur Dean and L. E. Marr as directors.

In 1959 the *Melrose Abbey*, a great favourite with her passengers, was sold to Greek owners after thirty years service, and in March that year the *Bolton Abbey* was the first vessel to call at the newly reconstructed Riverside Quay. She was joined by her sister ship a new *Melrose Abbey* and in 1962 the fleet comprised the *Bolton Abbey*, *Melrose Abbey*, *Darlington*, *Harrogate*, *Leeds*, *Selby*, *Wakefield*, *Whitby Abbey*, the *York*, a refrigerated vessel used as relief on the Copenhagen run, and three dumb lighters.

The *Fountains Abbey* caught fire in the North Sea in February that year with the loss of two of her 22 crew. After towing to Amsterdam she was scrapped and temporarily replaced on the Goole-Hamburg run by the *Rijsbergen*.

In June 1965 the m.v. *Leeds* began a lift-on lift-off service between Hull and Rotterdam with two sailings a week each way. The *Wakefield* was added to the service in 1966 and the m.v. *Melrose Abbey* and m.v. *Bolton Abbey* were also introduced to increase the sailings to five each way. Both the latter had been lengthened by the insertion of a 52ft prefabricated section amidships and could take containers, flats and other unit loads as well as general cargo and 88 passengers.

New container berths were available at Alexandra Dock in 1967 and the vessels moved there from Riverside Quay. There was now a total of seven vessels in the fleet, *Bolton Abbey*, *Melrose Abbey*, *Leeds*, *Wakefield*, *York*, *Darlington*, and *Whitby Abbey*.

E.W.L. took over the Goole-Copenhagen service of the British Railways Board and in 1968 purchased the *Kirkham Abbey* and *Byland Abbey* which were repainted in Wilson's livery, and renamed *Ariosto* and *Angelo*. They supplemented the joint service with DFDS which employed the *Aaro*, *Borodino*, *Friesia* and *Ficaria*, between Hull and Denmark.

Excessive competition and losses as a result of a depression in trade had resulted in the restructuring of AHL in 1957. The pooling of resources and a centralised control of commercial policy on rates and services had still however failed to establish stability and profitability. In 1971, then with only four vessels *Melrose Abbey*, *Bolton Abbey*, *Leeds*, and *Wakefield*, the company was closed down after failing to find a buyer. The peak of performance was reached in the 1950s but by 1967 there was a trading loss of £400,000 largely due to the inefficiency of old-fashioned cargo-handling methods.

The *Leeds* and *Wakefield* were sold to Medships Ltd. for £105,000 to operate out of Ipswich.

Since the war, the whole of the British shipping industry suffered from dock labour troubles, the port of Hull perhaps more severely than most. This only exacerbated the effects of international difficulties and rendered British companies less competitive because of higher handling costs and frequent delays.

In 1957 every vessel in the Wilson fleet had radar except for the *Spero* (built in 1922) sold for scrapping two years later. On 15 September 1957 the sailing of the *Sacramento* was delayed six days owing to the epidemic of Asian flu which was raging at the time. Thirty of her crew were affected and no replacements could be found. The American trade which had been inaugurated by ss *Othello* on 30 January 1875 came to end on 30 August 1961 when the *Domino* completed discharging her cargo in New York. Adverse trading conditions rendered the North Atlantic route no longer viable. In February 1964 the *Livorno* returned from Cyprus with a cargo of self-loading rifles in need of repair. Thirty-nine guns were found to be missing no doubt extracted by one of the terrorist groups active in that troubled Mediterranean island.

The majority of Wilson vessels accommodated twelve passengers in six double berths in considerable luxury in addition to their main cargo-carrying activity. In 1960 with a fleet of some 33 ships EWL were operating services from Hull, London, Liverpool, Manchester, Middlesbrough, Newcastle, Aberdeen, Swansea, Newport, Antwerp, Dunkirk etc. to and from Norway, Sweden, Denmark, the Baltic States, Poland, Portugal, the Mediterranean, Adriatic and Levant ports, Egypt, India, Pakistan, Canada and the USA and the Great Lake ports.

On the death of J. R. Fewlass in February 1959, E.W.L., now being part of Ellerman Lines, the company joined the other lines in the group under the chairmanship of A. F. Hull. Col. G. W. Bayley,[35] O.B.E., E.R.D., C.L. Small, P. G. Staniforth and E. Brown comprised the Hull Board, Col. Bayley being managing director.

A considerable development and restructuring of Wilson's business took place in the 1960's. Key Warehousing and Transport a subsidiary acquired in 1963 moved to modern premises in Marfleet in 1967 and in 1965 the Company's London agents the United Shipping Co. moved to Mariner House, Pepys Street, adjacent to the Port of London Authority headquarters.

Wilson's Stores Dept. held stores for the whole fleet and supplied many other shipping companies too, including the Ellerman Group vessels. A Workshop Department, formed originally to service the Wilson fleet, included shipwrights, sailmakers, joiners, carpenters, blacksmiths, tinners, plumbers, and ship's riggers. Castle and Co. William Street, Holderness Road, the nautical instrument makers and adjusters (also agents for Schermuly pyrotechnics) remained as a valuable 'technical branch' continuing the tradition of self-sufficiency within the firm, which had been so much a feature of the old Wilson organisation. Tranby Printers Ltd. formerly the Wilson Line Printing Works moved to new premises in Springfield Way, Anlaby, equipped with all the latest machinery. W.B.A. Timber Handling Co. Ltd. which was jointly owned with Brown Atkinson offered a comprehensive service to importers, but did not last long. Following the Devlin Report and decasualisation of dockworkers Wilson's became one of the biggest employers of dock labour in the country with a permanent workforce of over 1200 men. EWL had acquired Easons travel Agency in 1965 and two years later began operating Castlecraft dealing in yachts, dinghies and accessories for the small boat enthusiast.

An Agency Department handled vessels of many famous shipping lines when visiting Hull, a total of over 600 ships per annum of all kinds being dealt with in the late 1950s, including vessels of: Ellerman City Line; Hall Line; Ellerman Papayanni Line; Westcott and Laurance; Cunard; P & O; British India; Shaw, Saville and Albion; Bibby Line; Christian Salvesen etc. and later on also the Port Line.

In 1966 the regular fleet comprised 26 ships augmented by a number of chartered vessels. There was still a weekly service to Oslo and Oslofjord ports and a fortnightly service to Stavanger, Bergen and Trondheim. A weekly service also operated from London to Oslo and from Grimsby to Kristiansund S., Skien and Porsgrunn. Direct weekly services were maintained to Gothenburg from Hull and also to Malmo, Helsingborg and Halmstad and in conjunction with Svea Line from Hull and London to Norrköping, Stockholm and Gefle.

It may be noted that as early as 1908 a joint service between Wilson and Svea line had been established on the Norrköping/Stockholm — Hull/London routes.

May 1966 saw the formation of England Sweden Line a consortium of Svea Line, Swedish Lloyd and Ellerman's Wilson Line to provide frequent and regular sailings for passengers, cars and containerised cargoes between Hull and Gothenburg and London and Gothenburg. A vessel was placed under construction to the order of each constituent company intended to achieve a weekly quota of over 3500 passengers, nearly 1000 cars and some 10,000 tons of cargo. Wilson's commissioned the m.v. *Spero* to be built by Cammell-Laird[36] at Birkenhead with access for drive-on, drive-off movement of containers, flats and trailers and accommodation for 408 passengers in one class. There was space for 100 cars and those carrying four fare-paying passengers were loaded free. A one-way ticket excluding meals was £6.00 per person. *Spero* (the third of her name) was launched 5 May 1966 by Mrs. G. W. Bayley wife of the managing director and finally entered service 31 August after a delay of some three weeks at the builders. In the meantime the m.v. *Saga* the first of the consortium's vessels to enter the new service had left Gothenburg on her maiden voyage on the 6 May. During the wait for the completion of *Spero*, the m.v. *Salerno* (carrying cars and containers but not passengers), operated in conjunction with the Swedish vessel. The *Svea* was the third vessel which completed the trio of vessels in the England Sweden Line.

The captain chosen to be master of EWL's prestigious vessel, the most luxurious vessel ever built for them, costing some £2 million pounds and with lavish accommodation for her passengers, was David 'Ginger' Stokes, a Wilson Line veteran. He had joined the company as a cadet in 1921 and had enrolled at *Eldorado* the large warehouse in Bailey's yard, in the vicinity of Wilson's offices in Commercial Road, which functioned as a training school for cadets. Stokes had been awarded the OBE for activities in the ball-bearing run and was given the command (shared with Capt. Briggs) of Wilson's most expensive vessel and the first to establish regular container services from the UK. The new drive-on drive-off vessels of course needed different dockside facilities from traditional cargo vessels and new terminals were built at Hull, London and Gothenburg for the service.

That at Hull was officially opened by Barbara Castle, who was then the Minister for Transport.

In February 1967 the traditional green hull of the Wilson fleet

*The SS **Aaro** (1909), first vessel on the Humber equipped with wireless.*

which *Spero* wore was changed to light grey with white super-structure so as to more clearly resemble the white hulled *Svea* and *Saga*, and the three vessels had all the appearance of cruise liners. The whole idea of luxury ocean travel was heavily promoted so as to encourage the highest possible interest among the public and in the Spring of 1967 mini-cruises in the *Spero* were advertised and repeated again in the Autumn. Capt. Stokes after a long and distinguished career retired in December the following year.

The s.s. *Borodino* a popular ship with a crew of 51 and accommodation for 37 first class passengers was withdrawn from service in 1967. Two years later also saw the sale of the steamship *Volo* the last of the post-war rapid rebuild programme and one of eight in its class, the *Bravo, Carlo, Leo, Malmo, Silvio, Tinto* and *Truro*. All were essentially prewar in conception and were really obsolescent almost as soon as they entered service. Each had carried twelve passengers, who received a great deal of personal attention and were well provided for despite the primarily cargo-carrying nature of the vessel. Built by Swan-Hunter, Hall Russell, Robbs and Grays they were mostly employed in the Scandinavian trade.

The last steamers in the Ellerman's Wilson fleet, the *Rollo* and the *Cicero* were sold in late 1970 to the Maldives for service in the Indian Ocean. Built at Leith in 1954 they were two of the most luxurious of their class ever to sail out of the Humber and were active in the Gothenburg and Stockholm trade until the m.v. *Spero* arrived on the scene. Sister ships of 2500 tons they accommodated twelve passengers each of whom had his own personal bathroom suite. They subsequently sailed from London/Felixstowe to the Eastern Mediterranean under the Westcott and Laurance flag.

Even before the *Spero* venture was launched Wilson's had shown Wilson's determination to develop a modern fleet equipped for rapid and efficient cargo-handling. Known as the S-class since all five vessels of the type had names beginning with that letter, the first m.v. *Salerno* entered service in December 1965. Built by Henry Robb at Leith she was placed under the command of Capt. G. G. Needham, then aged 43. Measuring 2000 tons deadweight cargo the diesel engines gave a speed of 13 knots and she could take on board general and containerised or palletised cargo as well as refrigerated containers. There were side-loading doors, both port and starboard, for driving cargo straight into the tweendecks. A bow thruster propeller facilitated berthing and docking. The seventeen officers and crew were all provided with single berth cabins.

Salerno (whose old namesake incidentally had been captured in Norway when the Germans invaded) was followed by the *Sorrento*, in 1967, then the *Salmo, Silvio* and finally in 1968 the *Sangro*. *Salmo* was launched 12 December 1966 by Mrs. P. G. Staniforth whose husband was shortly to retire after fifty-one years service with Wilson's.[37] The vessel's maiden voyage began on 7 April 1967 with Capt. A. K. Skelton as master.

In 1969 two new ro-ro vessels, with stern doors for direct access to the dockside, the *Destro* and *Domino* were ordered in Norway to replace the lift-on lift-off container ships in the Norwegian trades. Both were nearly 1600 tons and some 360 feet in length. The m.v. *Spero* withdrawn from the Gothenburg service inaugurated a Hull-Zeebrugge ro-ro service in April 1972 and passengers were again offered mini-cruises (starting at £13.50p) aboard this well apppointed vessel, with the attractions of Bruges, and easy access to Holland and France as an added incentive; *Domino*, newly launched at Drammen, replaced her on the Gothenburg route.

Arthur Lowe, Star of TVs 'Coronation Street' and 'Dad's Army', travelled on board the vessel dressed as John Bull to mark the start of the service — a particularly appropriate choice since his son was a cadet officer with Ellermans.

June 1972 saw the launch of m.v. *Hero* at the Leith yard of Robb-Caledon a stern-loading ro-ro vessel jointly owned by EWL and DFDS for the Hull to Esbjerg service, carrying bacon and dairy produce from Denmark. She was the first vessel to use the new ro-ro terminal of the British Transport Docks Board at King George Dock.

As another expression of the spirit of enterprise which so characterised the company in the late 1960s Humber Airways Limited was acquired in 1968 a year after its formation. This Grimsby based air-taxi organisation was placed under the direction of J. R. Fewlass who was also EWL's deputy general manager. Younger son of a former chairman, he joined the company in 1944 and succeeded R. H. Dales as general manager in October 1969. A Hull-London service was established in March 1970 flying Britten-Norman Islanders from Brough to Leavesden, near Watford, but the construction of the chimney at the Capper Pass smelting works, standing nearly 600ft high prevented further development of the service from Brough.

The service was transferred to Leconfield but this closed after a very short experimental period as Hull passengers were not prepared 'to go north to get south'!

In 1973 HAL established a base at Dyce (Aberdeen) and operated the first commercial flight from the new Humberside Airport at Kirmington in Lincolnshire, on the day it was opened 26 March 1974.

In late 1974 the Ellerman Group decided to expand Humber

*The **Castro** which was used to take weapons from Germany to the Irish insurgents in 1916.*

*The SS **Accrington** equipped as a rescue ship but still showing her AHL insignia on the funnel; Captain Greenhorn was master with Robert E. Dalgleish, chief officer.*

*Capt. David 'Ginger' Stokes (without hat) on the bridge of the **Hopewell**, one of the ball-bearing blockade runners, known to the Germans as the "Grey Ladies".*

*The m.v. **Spero** (1966); a luxurious cargo-passenger vessel offering a drive-on, drive-off service to Gothenburg and later to Zeebrugge.*

Airways by the acquisition of an existing front line helicopter company, North Sea Helicopters/Management Aviation Ltd., and also to establish a frequent and passenger carrying service serving the North Sea Oil Industry from Aberdeen and Shetland using well tried, rugged, fixed wing aircraft. Early in January 1978 the Ellerman Board in London made a sudden decision to pull out of aviation completely and the helicopter deal was cancelled, the hangar and the Islander and Aztec aircraft were sold and so were four Douglas Dakota D.C.3 aircraft, which had been purchased less than one month earlier. These were intended to take advantage of the Shetland North Sea oil boom with the intention of replacing them with more modern aircraft as the need arose.

In December 1972 Mr. D. F. Martin-Jenkins, Ellerman Group chairman and managing director had announced a major group reorganisation stating that "the existing group structure, based on historically evolved subsidiary companies was unsuitable for modern trading conditions." This followed a loss after tax of £2 million for the 1971 trading year and it was decided to reorganise on a decentralised divisional basis; the three trading divisions were:

1. *Ellerman City Liners*, the shipping division of Ellermans Lines Ltd. Based in London it took over the ownership and management of the trades and ships of The City Line Ltd. Glasgow; Ellerman and Bucknall Steamship Co. Ltd. London; Ellerman and Pappyanni Lines Ltd. Liverpool; Ellerman's Wilson Line Ltd. Hull; (Mediterranean trades only); Hall Line Ltd. Liverpool; John Bruce and Co. Ltd. Glasgow; Wescott and Laurance Line Ltd. London; Containerships Portugal and Containerships Italy.

2. *EWL* the transport division of Ellerman Lines Ltd; based in Hull and managing and operating the North Sea Services of Ellerman's Wilson Line Ltd. it was also to develop transport operations. It embraced The Antwerp Steamship Co. Ltd; Ellerman and Wilson Lines Agency Co. Ltd. (Trieste); Ellerman's Wilson Line Ltd. (except Mediterranean trades and some trading departments); C. Hassell and Son Ltd; Humber Airways Ltd; Humber Keyways Ltd; Key Warehousing and Transport Co. Ltd; Maritime Transportation Ltd; T. Llewellyn Davies Ltd. (Air Freight); E. W. L. Air Cargo, and the United Shipping Co. Ltd.

Col. Bayley was appointed Divisional Chief Executive with J. W. B. Fewlass, chairman; J. R. Fewlass as Deputy Chief Executive with special responsibility for finance, stevedoring etc. R. D. Dales was the Divisional Director responsible for shipping operations. J. R. Fewlass was the Divisional Director responsible for Humber Airways Ltd. and E.W.L. Air Cargo. D. I. Bayley was the Divisional Director responsible for forwarding.

3. *Ellerman Travel and Leisure*; to be responsible for merging the groups national and international travel and leisure interests, namely: Castlecraft (Hull); The City Line Travel Ltd; Easons Travel Agency Ltd; Ellerman Lines Safaris Ltd. (Kenya); Kentmere Club Ltd. (Kenya) and T. Llewellyn Davies Ltd. (Agency and Holdings).

In February 1973 the Esbjerg service, still using m.v. *Hero* was transferred to Grimsby. 1974 saw a joint venture between EWL and the Swedish Roto Line between Felixstowe and Norway employing the ro-ro vessels m.v. *Valerie*, m.v. *Vallmo*, and m.v. *Vallann*. January 1973 saw the withdrawal of m.v. *Spero* from active service, she had never fulfilled the high hopes of a profitable cargo-passenger trade, and was sold to the Maritime Co. of Lesbos, Greece. She sailed from Hull under her new name of *Sappho* bound for Piraeus and a regular service between Piraeus, Chios and Lesbos. It was decided to increase the cargo-carrying capacity of m.v. *Hero* by some 40% when early in 1976 she entered Amsterdam for the insertion of a 25 metre section. She was able to re-enter service on 8 September 1976. This vessel was jointly owned with D.F.D.S. (U.K.), 50% each.

In 1970 four of the vessels built by Robb's in the 1950s were sold to the Maldives, following the *Teano* which had gone to the Indian Ocean in 1968. The *Aaro* also followed in 1972. After the major restructuring of Ellermans into divisional groups the *Rapallo*, *Salerno*, *Salmo*, *Sorrento*, *Sangro* and *Silvio* were all transferred to Ellerman City Liners.

January 1976 saw the last appearance of the *Jaroslov Dabrowski*, of the Polish Ocean Line. She had made no less than 559 voyages from Poland to the UK, on the Gydnia-Hull route from 1968. Her trading activities had been overseen by Wilson's as agents for all that time and she was the last coal burner to come into the port of Hull.

Wilson's had, prior to the 1914-18 War, a strong trade with Poland, and Czarist Russia. After the war the Russians would not allow foreign bottoms into the ports but the Polish trade was operated by Polish vessels of the Polish British Shipping Co. Ltd. of which Wilson's owned 25%. After the 1939-45 War, the vessels were wholly owned by the Poles but Wilson's retained the agency in Hull.

The only representative of Wilson's at the 1977 Silver Jubilee Spithead Review was the m.v. *Miranda* which was managed by

*The SS **Borodino**; discharging Danish produce on the Riverside Quay, Hull, 9th November 1959.*

them on behalf of the Department of Trade. She had gained considerable fame as 'mother ship' for the trawler fleets operating off Iceland during the recent 'Cod War'.

Trading conditions world-wide were increasingly difficult with over-capacity on almost all routes and an increasing number of vessels were leaving the British register to sail under "flags of convenience". This usually meant that vessels with mixed crews paid lower wages and could offer more favourable rates to merchants and traders. There was also a tendency to reduce manning levels — often quite drastically. A determination to maintain a hold on the traditional Scandinavian trade led to the commissioning of two 5,000 ton vessels from the shipbuilders Smiths Dock of Middlesbrough. Fewer but bigger units with larger cargo-carrying capacity would it was hoped enable EWL to trade efficiently and profitably. The *Cicero* was launched in 1978 followed by what sadly turned out to be the last vessel ever to be built for the E.W.L. fleet the *Cavallo* due for delivery in 1979. A ro-ro motor vessel intended for the Immingham-Scandinavian-Holland trade she proved to be a major headache for the firm. She was rejected on technical grounds and a writ was served on the builders for the return of the pre-delivery instalments and £7.2 million (plus interest and damages) to cover the cost of chartering a replacement. Previously her sister ship *Cicero* had been withdrawn from service for modifications, which took two months.

EWL sailings from the port of Hull had already ceased when on 29 September 1978 the *Destro* left King George dock en route for Norway, commanded by Capt. Frank Barnes, senior master of the line. The three vessels remaining in the fleet were incorporated into a new joint service with the Tor Line of Sweden and Fred Olsen Line of Norway, with the *Cavallo* later to join them, all sailing out of Immingham. A major contribution to the decision to pull out of Hull was the loss of m.v. *Hero* off Heligoland in November 1977 which resulted in the company having to charter ships to take the place of this profitable vessel. She had developed a severe list after taking in water in the engine room and trailer decks and one man was lost when *Hero* sank in the North Sea. *Destro* and *Domino* were sold to Italian owners in 1978 and the last glimpse of a Wilson vessel in Hull was the brief appearance of m.v. *Cicero* which came in for engine repairs to King George Dock in February 1980.

Not only did the Wilson Line reach its final demise in 1981 but in 1983 the whole of the Ellerman Group was for sale. It had losses of £9 million and for a number of years its brewing interests had probably been the most profitable and attractive part of the business. Bought by the hoteliers David and Frederick Barclay for £47 million, a management buy-out took place in 1985, followed in 1987 by sale to Trafalgar House plc (the owners of Cunard) to create Cunard Ellerman with Allan Kennedy of Cunard as Chairman.

The Wilson name still however survives in Sweden, at Gothenburg the home of Wilson and Co., one of Sweden's biggest shipping and forwarding agents. Founded in 1843 by John West Wilson who went to live there to run the Swedish end of the business for his father. Later becoming a naturalised citizen J. W. Wilson died unmarried in 1859, and the firm in due course, ended its direct links with the Wilson family and company and became completely independent.

The Wilson headquarters building at 1 Commercial Road also survives but is now turned over to leisure pursuits; what was the main concourse for the clerks is now an indoor bowling green. The company's old accountancy offices are occupied by Viking Radio, Hull's commercial radio station.[38]

Arthur G. Credland, October 1993

The old Wilson and Co. offices in Järntoget, Gothenburg; a firm founded by J. W. Wilson in 1843. (Photograph c.1925).

The Wilson Line offices, 1 Commercial Road, Hull, as they are today.

29

CHRONOLOGY

1792   Birth of Thomas Wilson at Hull. c.1806-13 apprenticed to Whitaker Wilkinson and Co., iron importers. A seven year span is usual.

1814   Married Susannah West, daughter of John West, wine and spirit merchant. David Wilson, their first child, born in 1815.

1823   Thomas Wilson, still a clerk.

c.1825   Beckinton, Wilson and Co., iron importers.

1831   Purchase of first elements of the fleet; the schooners *Swift* and *Peter and Jane*.

1833   Birth of Charles Henry Wilson.

1836   Wilson Hudson and Co. Purchase of the brig *Ivanhoe*. Birth of Arthur Wilson.

1841   Thomas Wilson, Sons and Co.

1851   Purchase of first steamer, P.S. *Courier*.

1855   *North Sea*, first vessel built for company at Earles Shipyard.

1861   Thomas Wilson relinquishes his direct hold on the firm.

1869   Thomas Wilson dies.

1870   Start of Adriatic trade.

1871   Start of Indian trade.

1873   Opening of Commercial Road premises.

1875   Start of N. American trade.

1878   Purchase of seven vessels of the defunct Brownlow Marsdin fleet.

1885/7   Joint advertising of N. American routes with Furness Line.

1890   Baccarat scandal at Tranby Croft, home of Arthur Wilson.

1891   Thomas Wilson, Sons and Co Ltd; becomes a private limited liability company.

1893   Purchase of three vessels of the Royal Exchange Co. of London for use in N. American trade.

1901   Purchase of Earles Shipyard by Charles Henry Wilson.

1903   Purchase of the Bailey and Leetham fleet; 23 vessels.

1903-4   Trade agreement with D.F.D.S. and formation of United Shipping Co.

1906   Formation of Wilson and North Eastern Railway Shipping Co.

1906   C. H. Wilson becomes Baron Nunburnholme of Warter Priory.

1907   Death of Lord Nunburnholme.

1909   Death of Arthur Wilson; E. Kenneth Wilson becomes Chairman.

1916   Heavy war losses; sale of company to Sir John Ellerman; in January to 1917 renamed Ellerman's Wilson Line.

1935   Formation of Associated Humber Lines.

1943-4   The 'ball-bearing' blockade runners.

1953   *Borodino* represents Ellerman's Wilson Line at the Coronation Spithead Review.

1965   m.v. *Salerno* launched, first of S-class vessels.

1966   Formation of England Sweden Line; launch of the m.v. *Spero*.

1968   Purchase of Humber Airways Ltd. (H.A.L.).

1970   Sale of the last two steamers in the fleet; *Rollo* and *Cicero*.

1971   Liquidation of A.H.L.

1973   Ellermans reorganised on a divisional basis; m.v. *Spero* withdrawn from service and sold abroad.

1977   Loss of the m.v. *Hero* off Heligoland.

1978   Sailings out of Hull ceased; vessels transferred to Immingham.

1978-9   m.v. *Cicero* and m.v. *Cavallo* launched.

1981   E.W.L. ceases operations.

1983   Ellerman Lines sold.

1987   Formation of Cunard-Ellerman.

1   Mrs. P. M. Pattinson, 'Thomas Wilson — a mystery resolved', *Banyan Tree*, no.8, Winter 1980-1, p.7. David Wilson (1737/8 — 1810) was married to Elizabeth Gray.

2   Susannah West (1794-1879) daughter of John West, wine and spirit importer; the marriage took place at Drypool Church, 1 September 1814. Fifteen children were born between 1815 and 1836.

3   John Hudson, chemist and druggist had premises at 28 Waterworks Street, Hull. A Thomas Hudson is listed in the trade directory in 1838 as agent for the Humber Union Steam Packet Company.

4   By 1851 this address was the office only and Thomas Wilson lived at Park Cottage (later called Park House) in Cottingham.

5   Perhaps John West Wilson, his second son.

6   Bound to Rostock she struck a rock on 5 March 1850 and was abandoned. Capt. Amery and his crew were picked up by the *Gazelle* and taken to Elsinore.

Charles Cammell went from Hull to Sheffield and in 1828 founded the firm of Charles Cammell and Co. It profited by the spread of the railways by producing rails, switches, carriage wheels and other equipment and in the 1860s became an important producer of armour plating. This resulted in the famous partnership of Cammell Laird which owned ordnance works at Coventry, coal mines, iron ore mines and smelting works at Workington, and a file factory at Odessa in Russia. It also owned an iron and steel works at Penistone and two steel works at Sheffield — the Cyclops and Grimethorpe. (Wilson's were important suppliers of iron to the Cyclops works). See *Builders of Great Ships* published 1959 by Cammell Laird and Co; and *Sheffield and Rotherham up-to-date*, 1899.

George Cammell, probably Charles' brother was Hull agent for the p.s. *Forfarshire*, the Hull-Dundee steam packet, famous for the rescue by Grace and William Darling when she was wrecked off the Farnes in 1838.

7   The story of the Scandinavian mail service is somewhat confused. According to other sources a certain P. Kleman of Gothenburg contracted with the Swedish and Norwegian governments in 1852 to carry their mail to Lowestoft and Grimsby. Six years later the contract was transferred to Thomas Wilson in Hull a service which continued until 1939 and the start of the war. Once peace resumed parcels were still taken to Gothenburg by sea but light items were transported by air.

Note that the p.s. *Courier* only appears on the Hull register in 1851 though the service began in 1850.

8   Joseph Armitage Wade and John Edward Wade of the firm of Richard Wade Sons and Co. timber merchants. A personal interest in a shipping company operating to Scandinavia and the Baltic the source of much valuable timber clearly gave them an advantage in obtaining supplies. It is worth noting that the trade directories up to 1851 were still describing Wilson's specifically as *iron* merchants as well as shipowners.

9   David Wilson (1815-1893), Thomas' eldest son, was born at 14 Salthouse Lane and lived in the family home at 31 Scale Lane, then 10 North Street (20 Charlotte Street) and latterly at Park House Cottingham. A close friend was Mark Firth a prominent Sheffield steel manufacturer whom he met through Wilson's iron importing business. He succeeded his brother as a director of the North Eastern Railway in 1873; was chairman of the Hull Steam Shipping Co. Ltd. chairman of the Cottingham Local Board and Gas Works, a Justice of the Peace and member of the East Riding County Council. Like his father he was a benefactor of the Hull Seamens and General Orphan Asylum. Along with his brothers Arthur and Charles he endowed the Wilson wing opened at the Hull Royal Infirmary in 1885 in memory of their father. He died unmarried at his Cottingham home. See *Hull Examiner* 17 May 1890, 'Men of Mark' no.7 and a memoir published in March 1893 recording the salient points of his life and details of his death and general service, printed by the *Eastern Morning News*, Hull.

10 Thomas Wilson (1792-1869); the funeral procession to his last resting place in the Hull General Cemetery, Spring Bank West, included men from the Earles shipyard and the orphans of the Seamens and General Orphan Asylum. Only a week earlier on 15 June he had chaired a committee meeting of the orphanage which he had supported generously over a number of years. In 1846 he was a director of the Hull Glass Works.

11 David was concentrating his efforts on the wine and spirit business; John had been established in Gothenburg since 1843 as the company agent, leaving the two youngest sons Charles and Arthur in charge of the Hull operation.

Marriage also played a part in the internal structure of the company; Harriet West Wilson, Thomas' eighth child, married William Eagle Bott, a merchant who became the firm's London agent. Elizabeth Gray Wilson the sixth child married Edward Rheam Sanderson; Oswald Sanderson, his nephew was to be a major figure in the future, see note 13.

[12] Arthur G. Credland, *Marine Painting In Hull through three centuries*, Hull, 1993, pp.120-3. The Walters painting is reproduced to accompany a description of the *Hindoo* in the *Illustrated London News*, 23 November 1872.

[13] Oswald Sanderson died in 1926. Chairman of the Wilson and North Eastern Railway Shipping Company, director of NER Shipping Co. of the NER Co. president of the Humber Conservancy Commission, director of Earles shipyard and director of the Suez Canal Co.

[14] A. G. Credland, *Iron and Steel Shipbuilding on the Humber – Earles of Hull*, Hull, 1982, pp.38-9; F. H. Pearson *The Early History of Hull Steam Shipping*, Hull 1896.

[15] The migrants were brought to Hull and then taken by rail to Liverpool which at the time dominated the transatlantic passenger trade.

[16] See note 14.

[17] William Barron *Old Whaling Days*, Hull, 1895.

[18] The capital was subscribed equally by the two partners.

[19] See note 14. *Earles of Hull*, pp.40-1. Henry Wilson Ringrose Smith in fact learned his trade as an engineer in the Earles yard.

[20] Charles Henry Wilson (1833-1907), first Baron Nunburnholme of Warter Priory. He had married Florence Wellesley, a great niece of the Duke of Wellington, in 1871 and they settled at Thwaite House in Cottingham. In 1878 he purchased Warter Priory with its 300 acre estate from Lord Muncaster. He had been Sheriff of Hull in 1870 and was elected member of parliament for Hull in 1874 and sat in the House of Commons until he received his peerage. Charles Henry Wilson left an estate of over £1 million.

[21] The Warter Priory estate passed through the hands of George Vestey and then in 1968 to the Guinness family; the house was demolished in 1972.

[22] Arthur Wilson, the youngest of Thomas' children was born in 1836. A detailed account of his household is given by Gertrude M. Attwood *The Wilsons of Tranby Croft*, Hull, 1988.

See also R. H. A. Currey, 'Mrs. Arthur Wilson', *The Hull Lady*, November, 1901, pp.25-30.

[23] Right Rev. Herbert Bury, *My Visit to Ruhleben*, London, 1917.

[24] D. P. Branigan 'The Saga of the Aud', *Yorkshire Life*, September 1972; Dr. J. E. de Courcy Ireland *The Mariners Mirror*, vol.67, no.4, Nov. 1981, p.383.

[25] William J. Allen, s.s. *Borodino* MFA No.6 *A short account of the Junior Army and Navy Stores with HM Grand Fleet Dec. 1914 – Feb. 1919*, London, n.d.

[26] His mother was Anne Reeves daughter of a local solicitor. He was taken to live in Caen, Normandy, aged seven, after the death of his father. (It is a matter of speculation whether Mrs. Ellerman was related to W. K. Reeves, architect of Savile Street, Hull, who in 1872 had prepared the designs for the Wilson's new headquarters at 1 Commercial Road.)

[27] For an announcement of the take-over see *Hull and Eastern Morning News*, Saturday 14 October, 1916.

[28] Edward Kenneth Wilson (1869 — 1947) son of Arthur Wilson, brother of Arthur Stanley, Muriel and Clive Harry Adolphus.

[29] Alan Wilkinson, *Geni on the line*, Hull, 1990; J. H. Chinnery *Fishing off Greenland; the voyage of the ss Arctic Prince 16 April – 7 October 1933*, Malet Lambert Local History Originals, vol.9, Hull 1982.

[30] B. B. Schofield and L. F. Martyn, *The Rescue Ships*, London, 1968.

[31] Ralph Barker *The Blockade Busters*, London 1976; Lawrie Kohler, B. E. M. *A Life at Sea*, pt.2, Malet Lambert Local History Originals, no.18, Hull 1984. Two of the gunboats were converted by Amos and Smith on the Albert dock, Hull.

In 1941 Wilson's and Co. provided many officers and crew for an attempt to bring home ten merchant vessels trapped in Gothenburg since the start of the war. The mission (Operation Performance) was not a success and resulted in heavy casualties.

[32] Herbert Stanley Holden joined Wilson's in 1889 and became company secretary after the Ellerman takeover; Managing Director 1927 and Chairman in 1933. He died 3 November 1946. J. W. Bayley was regional representative of the Ministry of War Transport for Humber and the Wash; Chairman of Ellerman Lines 1950.

[33] J. R. Fewlass Snr joined the company in 1931; secretary in 1933, assistant general manager and a director in 1940. Thereafter general manager and finally chairman. He died in February 1959.

34 Purchased from AHL by Wilson's in 1968 *Byland Abbey* and *Kirkham Abbey* were renamed *Angelo* and *Ariosto* respectively. Both were sold to the Maldives two years later.

35 Lt. Col. George Wyrill Bayley OBE, ERD, joined Ellerman's Wilson Line in 1933. Appointed to the board of Ellerman and Papayanni and Westcott and Laurance in 1969. Retired December 1977 as chairman and chief executive of EWL but continued as non-executive board member of Ellerman's until Summer 1978. He was succeeded as chairman and chief executive by Mr. T. D. Martin-Jenkins in January 1978.

36 An appropriate choice considering the early involvement with Charles Cammell.

37 Percy Garner Staniforth, joined the company during the First World War at the age of thirteen eventually becoming a director. He retired in 1966 after 51 years service and died in 1971.

38 The Commercial Road premises were opened in 1873 and the firm had moved into their splendid purpose-built offices (backing onto the Railway dock) from 3 Railway Street (between Castle Street and Wellington Street).

   From c.1846 the office was at 31 Scale Lane with Wilson and Voase, ship and insurance brokers and commission agents at 17 Bowlalley Lane. By 1848 Thomas Wilson was living at Cottingham, but the office address is again given as 14 Salthouse Lane. At 3 Railway Street in 1857 the company is also listed in the trade directories as agent to the North of Europe Steam Navigation Co. Railway Street was used as a refreshment room for employees after the Commercial Road establishment was opened and later became the Hull Peoples Café and Catering Co. Ltd. Commercial Road was vacated before the winding up operations of EWL were completed and latterly the office accommodation was in Lowgate and at the very end in Blackfriargate (Hull).

Sources not mentioned in the notes:

Anon 'The other four-fifths', *Port of Hull Journal*, vol.5, no.2, pp.13-21.

Anon, 'Wilson Line' *The Times Shipping Number* 1913 (reprinted from 'The Times', 13 Dec., 1912), pp.38-9.

Anon, 'Messrs. Thomas Wilson, Sons and Co. Limited', *The Mariner*, December 1894, pp.124-126.

Anon. 'Ellerman's Wilson Line', *Ellerman's on shore and afloat*, 30 September, 1969, no.7, pp.4-7.

Anon. 'Ellerman's Wilson Line Ltd.' Supplement to *The American and Commonwealth Visitor*, August 1953, pp.VIII-IX.

Anon. 'Messrs. Thomas Wilson, Sons, and Co. Ltd., Ship Owners' *Modern Hull*, Hull, 1893, pp.21-4.

Anon. 'Ellerman's Wilson Line', *Sea Breezes*, January 1955. pp.32-51.

N.R.P. Bonsor, *North Atlantic Seaway*, London, 1975-8, 5 vols.

Christopher Munday, 'Sea communications and the Norwegian fresh fish trade with England 1880-1913', *Sjofarts historiske Arbok*, Bergen Sjofartsmuseum, Bergen, 1985, pp.83-138.

THE WILSON LINE SAILING SHIP FLEET (1831-1854)

NAME FORMER NAMES	GROSS NET	LENGTH BREADTH DEPTH	BUILDER PLACE YEAR	OTHER DETAILS
OSWY	124	69.2 20.7 12.0	Whitby 1819	A brig bought in 1831, from Whitby. Sold to London owners on 18.5.1840.
PETER & JANE	85.5	65.5 18.0 10.0	N. Shields 1825	A schooner bought in 1831, from Newcastle. Sold to Whitby owners 6.5.1839.
SWIFT	100	61.0 16.6 11.0	Newcastle 1829	A schooner bought in 1831, from Newcastle. Sold to London owners on 14.6.1839.
IVANHOE	140	82.6 19.7 12.2	Goole 1837	A square rigged vessel built for T. Wilson. Sold to Stockton owners 16.1.1854.
CREST	345	95.5 23.6 17.2	Sunderland 1839	A square rigged vessel built for J. Hudson. Lost at sea 1847.
THOMAS RICKINSON	260	85.5 21.7 15.9	Whitby 1839	A snow rigged vessel bought from Whitby in 1840. Lost at sea 1847.
PATRIOT	93	79.6 17.6 11.1	Hull 1839	A schooner built for T. Wilson. Lost at sea 31.10.1858.
DWINA	121	67.5 17.9 11.9	Hull 1841	A schooner built for T. Wilson. Lost at sea 5.3.1850.
OSCAR	77	14.5 14.5 8.9	Hull 1847	A schooner built for T. Wilson. Lost at sea 1848.
WAVE	36	63.4 15.8 9.3	Hull 1848	A schooner built for T. Wilson. Lost at sea 19.12.1853.
SUSAN	220	91.1 21.3 14.3	Hull 1850	A brig built for T. Wilson. Sold to Montrose owners 19.1.1854.

THE WILSON LINE FLEET LIST IN CHRONOLOGICAL ORDER OF ENTRY INTO FLEET
THE STEAM-SHIP FLEET

NAME FORMER NAMES	GROSS NET	LENGTH BREADTH DEPTH	BUILDER PLACE YEAR	OTHER DETAILS
COURIER (PS)	245	175.8 21.8 12.1	T. Wingate Glasgow 1850	Bought 1851, from Hull & Leith Steam Packet Co. Sold 15.3.1854 to London owners. 10.7.1875, struck Emanuel Head, Holy Island, on passage Seaham — Aberdeen. Refloated after 30 minutes with assistance of a local tug and fishing boats but sank inside Holy Island Bar. 18.10.1875, sold by auction and subsequently scrapped.
SCANDINAVIAN *TASSO (1)	610 472	184.5 23.0 13.9	T. Wingate Lanark 1852	Renamed TASSO (1) 1870. Wrecked 14.3.1886, in Bommel fjord, nr Bergen, Norway. All crew saved.
BALTIC (1)	535 399	181.8 25.1 14.3	Denny Bros. Dumbarton 1854	Sold 14.11.1856 to British India Company. Wrecked on Alguada Reef 1863.
HUMBER	656 509	182.3 25.1 14.3	Denny Bros. Dumbarton 1854	Sold 12.9.1896 to Sig. Magnano, Genoa. Renamed MARIA ROSA. Scrapped February 1899.
IRWELL	812 656	223.2 26.3 15.5	M. Samuelson Hull 1854	Sold 5.10.1881 to W. G. Reincke, Windau, Russia. Renamed NORD SEE. Wrecked in the Baltic due to ice 17.3.1899.
NORTH SEA	614 450	208.0 26.0 18.0	Earle's Hull 1855	Wrecked 27.3.1859, near Agger Canal, Holmen, Jutland. All crew saved and a considerable amount of cargo was salved.
KINGSTON	372 289	167.0 21.0 13.0	Earle's Hull 1856	Lost Dec. 1860, wrecked on Hasbro' Sands or after collision in the vicinity. Left Gothenburg on 27.12.1860 for London. Between 2nd — 6th January wreckage marked KINGSTON was washed ashore.
NEVA	558 379	153.0 22.0 11.0	Earle's Hull 1856	Lost 25.11.1856, foundered 120 miles off the coast of Jutland. On passage Cronstadt — Hull.
ATLANTIC	1309 1111	254.6 30.4 24.1	Earle's Hull 1857	Sold 28.3.1860, to J. Moss, Liverpool. Then to Haroutioun Sorgondje, London. Sold 1889, to Idarei Massousieh, Turkey. Renamed KAPLAN. Lost in collision March 1898.

ss. *NERO (1)* **1868-1905**

ENGINE:	2 cyl. compound
MADE BY:	C. & W. Earle, Hull.
POWER:	95 NHP
1 BOILER	95lb per sq.in.
SPEED:	9 knots
SERVICE:	North Sea, Lower Baltic.
PASSENGERS:	12 — 1st Class.

ss. *ROLLO (1)* **1870-1909**

ENGINE:	4 cyl. compound
MADE BY:	C. & W. Earle, Hull.
POWER:	195 NHP
2 BOILERS	75lb per sq.in.
SPEED:	11½ knots
SERVICE:	Norway.
PASSENGERS:	170 — 1st Class.
	28 — 2nd.
	597 — 3rd.

ss. *YEDDO* 1871-1907

ENGINE:	2 cyl. compound
MADE BY:	C. & W. Earle, Hull.
POWER:	250 NHP
2 BOILERS	90lb per sq.in.
SPEED:	9½ knots
SERVICE:	Mediterranean, Black Sea.
PASSENGERS:	4 — 1st Class.

ss. *HIDALGO (1)* 1872-1907

ENGINE:	2 cyl. compound
MADE BY:	Earle's Shipbuilding & Eng. Co. Ltd. Hull.
POWER:	140 NHP
2 BOILERS	120lb per sq.in.
SPEED:	9 knots
SERVICE:	Mediterranean, Black Sea.
PASSENGERS:	16 — 1st Class.

NAME FORMER NAMES	GROSS NET	LENGTH BREADTH DEPTH	BUILDER PLACE YEAR	OTHER DETAILS
BALTIC (2)	631 525	185.0 26.6 16.6	Earle's Hull 1858	Wrecked 23.6.1861, on Rickmans Ground. Dago Island. On passage Hull — Cronstadt.
ARCTIC	674 559	192.6 27.0 16.0	Earle's Hull 1859	Wrecked 4.10.1860, off Lemvig on the coast of Jutland. On passage Hull — St. Petersburg. 8 lives lost.
ARGO (1)	750 493	210.5 30.3 16.2	Earle's Hull 1860	Sold 13.1.1896, to J. J. Sitges Freres, Spain. Renamed NUEVO CORREO DE ALICANTE. Foundered 12.3.1913 off Heraklea. As KASSOS (Greek).
BOTHNIA	723 615	203.8 27.2 16.0	Earle's Hull 1860	Lost at sea January 1861, circumstances unknown. Last seen passing Elsinore 4.1.1861. Posted missing with crew of 22.
PACIFIC *MALMO (1)	724 575	203.8 27.2 16.0	Earle's Hull 1860	Renamed MALMO (1) 1888. Sold 14.5.1900, W. H. Stott Liverpool. (Spartan Chief S. S. Co.) Sold 19.6.1907. to Aberdeen owners as a Hulk.
ALBION *ALBANO (1)	1050 772	245.2 29.0 17.0	M. Samuelson Hull 1861	Renamed ALBANO (1) 12.6.1880. Sold 11.11.1896, to Marine Association. Wrecked near Kemi Finland 26.9.1897.
HEBE	968 789	220.0 29.0 21.0	Earle's Hull 1861	Wrecked 26.11.1861, 8 pm on a reef at Fuhland, Gothland, on 3rd voyage. All passengers and crew were rescued with assistance from ashore.
HERO (1)	899 764	224.3 29.2 15.7	Earle's Hull 1861	Sold 19.4.1862 to Wm. Whitworth, Manchester, agent for the U.S.A. Confederate States, used as a blockade runner during Civil War. Resold various owners Australia & New Zealand. 1891 hulked in New Caledonia.
JUNO (1)	1060 869	246.2 29.5 21.2	M. Samuelson Hull 1861	Sold 8.9.1863 to Wm. Whitworth, Manchester, agent for the U.S.A. Confederate States used as a blockade runner during Civil War. 1899 sold as JUNON by Compagnie de Marseilles de Nav. for scrapping.
NORTH EASTERN	583 475	190.5 26.8 15.4	Richardson Low Walker 1861	Bought 18.4.1863, from W. Gray, Sunderland. Lost Nov. 1864. Foundered in the Baltic. All 20 crew were lost. At the time shipping in the Baltic was experiencing severe gales and icing conditions.

NAME FORMER NAMES	GROSS NET	LENGTH BREADTH DEPTH	BUILDER PLACE YEAR	OTHER DETAILS
ODER	694 556	200.0 27.5 15.0	Earle's Hull 1861	Lost 16.10.1875. Foundered in the North Sea. In position 56.14'N x 04.12'E. Whilst on passage Liverpool-Gothenburg.
DIDO (1)	1409 1062	278.0 30.4 21.8	Earle's Hull 1862	Sold 20.8.1894, to Earle's Shipbuilding Co. Then to W. Pitts for Scrapping.
OUSE	725 601	214.3 28.8 14.8	Earle's Hull 1862	Wrecked 31.5.1867, on the Island of Thisted, near Holman Light, Jutland. On passage Hull — Stettin — Riga. All passengers and crew were landed safely.
TRENT	717 590	213.8 28.7 14.8	Earle's Hull 1862	Wrecked 7.6.1862. Lost on her maiden voyage, on Neckmans Ground, off Dago Island, whilst on passage from Hull-Cronstadt.
UNITED SERVICE	583 472	190.5 27.4 —	Richardson Low Walker 1862	Bought 28.11.1864, from W. Gray, Sunderland. Lost at sea about 12.12.1866, foundered in severe gale. On passage Stettin — Hull. Left shelter of Scaw 11th December, later seen under sail, (possible engine breakdown). Posted missing lost with all hands.
CLIO (1)	1107 898	234.0 30.6 19.9	Earle's Hull 1864	Stranded 7.12.1866, on the west coast, of Jutland. Salved after 18 months, repaired in Scotland. Sold 13.11.1868, to Bailey & Leetham of Hull. Lost 23.7.1869, in collision with NIOBE, in thick fog off Gothland. 16 crew were lost including the Master.
JUNO (2)	1104 896	234.0 30.6 19.9	Earle's Hull 1864	Stranded 1.1.1867, on the Prussian coast. Driven ashore in severe blizzard, on passage Danzig — Antwerp. All 23 crewmen rescued.
SAPPHO (1)	1102 895	234.1 30.6 19.9	Earles Hull 1864	Sold 17.3.1898, to H. Pukne, Riga. Scrapped 1904.
APOLLO (1)	1336 1125	251.6 32.1 20.5	Earle's Hull 1865	Lost 7.3.1882, in Bay of Biscay. In collision with the French ship ss. PRECURSEUR whilst on passage Hull — Palermo.
CALYPSO (1)	1334 865	251.4 32.1 20.5	Earle's Hull 1865	Sold 1.9.1902 to Bruzzo Bros. For scrapping at Genoa.
MILO	1057 683	240.5 29.2 15.0	London & Glasgow Glasgow 1865	Sold 7.7.1904 to Bells Asia Minor Co. Liverpool. Scrapped 1918.

ss. *ROMEO* 1881-1918

ENGINE:	2 cyl. compound
MADE BY:	Earle's Shipbuilding & Eng. Co. Ltd. Hull.
POWER:	350 NHP
2 BOILER	80lb per sq.in.
SPEED:	12½ knots
SERVICE:	Norway.
PASSENGERS:	38 — 1st Class.
	18 — 2nd.
	780 — 3rd.

ss. *DRACO (1)* 1882-1905

ENGINE:	3 cyl. Triple expansion
MADE BY:	Earle's Shipbuilding & Eng. Co. Ltd. Hull.
POWER:	140 NHP
2 BOILERS	90lb per sq.in.
SPEED:	9 knots
SERVICE:	Mediterranean, Black Sea.
PASSENGERS:	Nil.

ss. _MARTELLO_ 1884-1910

ENGINE:	3 cyl. Triple expansion
MADE BY:	Earle's Shipbuilding & Eng. Co. Ltd. Hull.
POWER:	400 NHP
4 BOILERS	150lb per sq.in.
SPEED:	12 knots
SERVICE:	North America.
PASSENGERS:	8 — 1st Class. Immigrants as required.

ss. _ELDORADO (3)_ 1886-1913

ENGINE:	3 cyl. Triple expansion
MADE BY:	Earle's Shipbuilding & Eng. Co. Ltd. Hull.
POWER:	250 NHP
2 BOILERS	150lb per sq.in.
SPEED:	15 knots
SERVICE:	Norway.
PASSENGERS:	106 — 1st Class.
	16 — 2nd.
	312 — 3rd.

NAME FORMER NAMES	GROSS NET	LENGTH BREADTH DEPTH	BUILDER PLACE YEAR	OTHER DETAILS
BARON *HAMBRO*	574 439	209.0 25.2 14.5	Lungley Deptford 1861	Bought 26.6.1866. from Harington, London. Sold 22.6.1871 to G. N. Todd London. Sold 1899, to P. P. Gourgy, Odessa. Renamed *TARAS BUOLBA*. Sold 1922, renamed *OLGA METHINITY* (Russian), Scrapped 1923.
BRAVO (1)	1076 695	240.1 29.2 15.9	London & Glasgow Glasgow 1866	Sold 29.9.1904, to Bells Asia Minor Co. Liverpool. Scrapped 1907, at Alexandria.
ECHO	787 599	220.6 27.6 16.5	Richardson Low Walker 1863	Bought 1866, from foreign owners. Lost at sea 24.10.1869, during severe gale in the North Sea. On passage Cronstadt — Hull. Posted missing lost with all 18 crew.
HERO (2)	1034 671	229.1 30.6 20.8	Earle's Hull 1866	Badly damaged in collision 22.6.1895, with Lamport & Holt's *BESSEL* in the English Channel. Sold to Earle's 9.9.1895. Who subsequently sold her to W. Pitts for scrap.
SWALLOW	319 217	172.5 21.2 12.5	Earle's Hull 1857	Bought 23.3.1867 from Depledge, Hull. Sold 17.8.1868, to Grandchamp, France. 1907 sold as *HIRONDELLE* by Worms et Cie, Dieppe, for scrapping probably at Dunkirk.
CATO (1)	1094 700	245.4 29.5 16.2	London & Glasgow Glasgow 1867	Sold 11.6.1907, to Aga Mohamed Jaffer Bussorah, Turkish Arabia. Renamed *JAFFARI*. Scrapped in 1922.
FIDO (1)	954 741	217.8 29.0 16.8	Earle's Hull 1867	Sold 21.12.1901, to King & Sons Ltd. For scrapping.
OTTO (1)	1052 815	224.6 29.9 15.5	Earle's Hull 1867	Lost, 16.8.1892, in collision off Lappegrund, whilst on passage Danzig-Grimsby.
GOZO	1008 783	217.8 29.0 16.8	Earle's Hull 1868	Sold 1.12.1899, to M. Lawson & Co. Workington. For Scrapping.
INO	1016 814	230.0 29.0 19.6	Earle's Hull 1868	Wrecked 27.12.1871, on Paternoster Rocks off the coast of Sweden. Whilst on passage Hull-Riga.

NAME FORMER NAMES	GROSS NET	LENGTH BREADTH DEPTH	BUILDER PLACE YEAR	OTHER DETAILS
NERO (1)	1083 697	220.4 31.1 15.6	Earle's Hull 1868	Sold 12.7.1905, N. P. Cosmetto, Piraeus. Renamed STADION. Hulked 1910 at Piraeus.
PLATO (1)	1013 814	230.0 29.0 19.6	Earle's Hull 1868	Lost at sea 24.10.1870, in the Bay of Biscay, circumstances unknown, wreckage bearing the name PLATO was found on the coast of Penmarch.
JUNO (3)	1083 866	220.6 31.0 16.0	Earle's Hull 1869	Lost at sea 23.5.1871, circumstances unknown. Posted missing lost with all hands.
KELSO (1)	1050 839	220.7 31.1 15.6	Earle's Hull 1869	Badly damaged by fire 4.6.1900, On passage Hull — Stockholm. Towed into Gothenburg, sold for scrap.
LEO (1)	1083 704	220.6 31.1 15.6	Earle's Hull 1869	Sold 7.2.1910, to Forth Shipbreaking Co. For scrapping at Boness.
ORLANDO (1)	1581 1047	260.0 32.2 19.0	Earle's Hull 1869	Sold 5.8.1909, to Paul Castinie, Oran (French). Renamed ALGERIE. Wrecked Canea 1924 as VELLISSARIOUS (Turkish).
ERATO (1)	1522 972	252.4 34.8 17.5	Humphry & Pearson Hull, 1870	Sold 10.10.1903, to Gebr. Seeburg, Riga, Latvia. Renamed GRAF TOLSTOI. Scrapped in Holland 1926, as HERTHA HENCKALL (German).
QUITO	1526 1172	253.4 34.8 17.5	Earle's Hull 1870	Wrecked 13.1.1891 on Nidizin Rocks, Lidingen, Sweden on passage Riga — Hull.
ROLLO (1)	1568 1032	260.0 32.3 19.0	Earle's Hull 1870	Sold 10.9.1909, to The Nordenhamer S. B. For scrapping at Einwarden.
THOMAS WILSON	1377 732	253.4 34.8 17.5	Earle's Hull 1870	Sold 26.10.1901, to Gebr. Seeburg, Riga, Latvia. Renamed GENERAL RADETSKY. Foundered in the North Sea 13.11.1909.
COMO (1)	1497 990	272.6 32.0 17.7	Earle's Hull 1871	Sold 26.1.1905, to H. I. Ambecht, Holland. For scrapping at Rotterdam.

ss. _COLORADO_ (1) 1887-1908

ENGINE:	3 cyl. Triple expansion
MADE BY:	Amos and Smith, Hull
POWER:	450 NHP
2 BOILERS	160lb per sq.in.
SPEED:	12 knots
SERVICE:	North America.
PASSENGERS:	26 — 1st Class.

ss. _OHIO_ 1887-1904

ENGINE:	2 cyl. compound
MADE BY:	D. Rowan, Glasgow
POWER:	500 NHP
3 BOILERS	80lb per sq.in.
SPEED:	10½ knots
SERVICE:	North America.
PASSENGERS:	28 — 1st Class.
	1200 — 3rd.

ss. *DOURO* 1889-1929

ENGINE: 3 cyl. Triple expansion
MADE BY: T. Richardson & Sons Hartlepool
POWER: 200 NHP
2 BOILERS 160lb per sq.in.
SPEED: 10 knots
SERVICE: Mediterranean, Black Sea.
PASSENGERS: Nil.

ss. *POLO (1)* 1889-1910

ENGINE: Quad 4 cyl.
MADE BY: Earle's Shipbuilding & Eng. Co. Ltd. Hull.
POWER: 68 NHP
1 BOILER 90lb per sq.in.
SPEED: 9½ knots
SERVICE: Home Trade.
PASSENGERS: Nil.

NAME FORMER NAMES	GROSS NET	LENGTH BREADTH DEPTH	BUILDER PLACE YEAR	OTHER DETAILS
URBINO (1)	1535 1230	272.0 32.1 16.0	Schlesinger Newcastle 1871	Wrecked 9.1.1879, entrance to Cadiz. Whilst on passage Hamburg-Cadiz.
VIRAGO	1809 1454	282.0 34.8 19.0	Earle's Hull 1871	Wrecked 1882, on Isle of Alderney Whilst on passage to Constantinople — Odessa. Passed Dover 1.6.1882.
WALAMO	1832 1466	283.0 34.8 19.8	Earle's Hull 1871	Foundered 16.9.1873, off the Dogger Bank. After cargo had shifted. On passage Hull — Cronstadt.
XANTHO	1807 1454	282.0 34.8 19.6	Earle's Hull 1871	Lost 24.6.1884, in collision off the Island of Gothland with German vessel s.s. *VALUTA*. On passage Cronstadt — Hull.
YEDDO	1850 1471	283.2 34.8 19.8	Earle's Hull 1871	Sold 21.1.1907, To T. Ward For scrapping at Widnes.
ZENO	1490 1163	272.6 32.0 18.0	Earle's Hull 1871	Lost 13.5.1873, by explosion, 202 miles S. W. of the Scilly Isles. Whilst on passage Cardiff — Port Said. No lives lost.
COLOMBO	2624 1650	331.1 36.7 27.1	Humphry & Pearson Hull 1872	Posted missing in N. Atlantic January 1876, Left Hull for New York 3.12.1876. Last spoken to 16.12.1876 in position 36 N x 35 W.
HIDALGO (1)	1581 1220	272.6 32.0 17.8	Earle's Hull 1872	Sold 14.1.1907, to T. W. Ward, Sheffield, For scrapping.
HINDOO (1)	3257 2361	379.8 37.1 21.1	Lawrie Glasgow 1872	Foundered 22.2.1880, in N. Atlantic, in position 41.51′N x 41.06′W, Left New York for Hull on 11th, February 1880. During the voyage grain cargo shifted and vessel became unmanageable, funnel was carried away and decks swept clear. The 1st & 2nd mates, quartermaster and 32 seamen were lost overboard. On 22nd, the derelict was sighted by the ss. *ALEXANDRIA* which rescued the remaining 53 crew and passengers.

NAME FORMER NAMES	GROSS NET	LENGTH BREADTH DEPTH	BUILDER PLACE YEAR	OTHER DETAILS
OTHELLO (1)	2479 1939	316.0 36.1 27.1	Earle's Hull 1872	Sold 1.6.1895 to C. Garnett For scrapping.
PALERMO (1)	1635 1317	270.0 32.6 23.1	Schlesinger Newcastle 1872	Sold 15.2.1900, to Fratello Grerboz, Fiume, Scrapped 1904.
RINALDO (1)	1663 1284	279.0 32.1 18.7	Earle's Hull 1872	Stranded 25.1.1908, near Moen Island. Refloated and sold 11.4.1908, for scrapping, at Copenhagen.
ARROW (TUG)	85 25	91.3 18.1 9.1	Middlesbrough 1864	Bought 16.5.1873, from Wm. Cooper Grimsby. Sold 31.1.1877, to W. & T. Jolliffe, Liverpool. Scrapped in 1883.
ELDORADO (1)	3332 2157	387.3 39.1 19.4	Earle's Hull 1873	Sold 19.2.1878, to Gray Dawes & Co. Glasgow. Wrecked 1885, near Peniche, On passage London — Colombo.
NAVARINO	3400 2189	389.0 38.8 19.7	Earle's Hull 1873	Sold 5.1.1878, to Gray Dawes & Co. Glasgow. Scrapped 1895.
ANGELO (1)	1547 978	258.8 33.6 18.2	Humphry & Pearson Hull, 1874	Sold 7.2.1906, to White & White, For scrapping.
CAMEO	1244 802	245.0 31.0 17.3	Earle's Hull 1876	Sold 12.9.1908 to T. W. Ward, Preston. For scrapping.
ZERO (1) (TUG) **SAMBO*	77 —	80.0 17.1 8.3	Schlesinger & Davis Wallsend 1876	Renamed *SAMBO* 1896. Scrapped 4.1.1905 by Amos & Smith Hull.
DOMINO (1)	937 599	225.4 28.2 14.7	Schlesinger & Davis Newcastle 1877	Sold 14.5.1905, to T. B. Stott Liverpool. (Spartan Chief S. S. Co.) Sold 1912, renamed *SIGNE* (Swedish) Sold 1913, renamed *AGNES* (Finnish) Sold 1923, renamed *GEORGE.S* (Greek) Sold 1926, renamed *LUISA* (Italian) Scrapped in Italy 1832.

ss. *ARIOSTO (1)* 1890-1910

ENGINE:	3 cyl. Triple expansion
MADE BY:	Earle's Ship building & Eng. Co. Ltd. Hull.
POWER:	400 NHP
2 BOILERS	160lb per sq.in.
SPEED:	14½ knots
SERVICE:	Norway.
PASSENGERS:	53 — 1st Class.
	24 — 2nd.
	826 — 3rd.

ss. *VOLO (1)* 1890-1924

ENGINE:	3 cyl. Triple expansion
MADE BY:	Amos and Smith, Hull.
POWER:	200 NHP
2 BOILERS	160lb per sq.in.
SPEED:	12½ knots
SERVICE:	Lower Baltic.
PASSENGERS:	16 — 1st Class.

ss. *BRUNO* 1892-1909

ENGINE:	3 cyl. Triple expansion
MADE BY:	Earle's Shipbuilding & Eng. Co. Ltd. Hull.
POWER:	170 NHP
2 BOILERS	152lb per sq.in.
SPEED:	13½ knots
SERVICE:	Hamburg.
PASSENGERS:	10 — 1st Class. 58 — 3rd.

ss. *FINLAND* 1893-1917

ENGINE:	3 cyl. Triple expansion
MADE BY:	Earle's Shipbuilding & Eng. Co. Ltd. Hull.
POWER:	152 NHP
2 BOILERS	160lb per sq.in.
SPEED:	9 knots
SERVICE:	Mediterranean, Black Sea.
PASSENGERS:	Nil.

NAME FORMER NAMES	GROSS NET	LENGTH BREADTH DEPTH	BUILDER PLACE YEAR	OTHER DETAILS
LEPANTO (1)	2310 1871	305.0 36.1 26.0	Earle's Hull 1877	Lost 7.1.1898, in collision with ss. *KNIGHT OF ST. GEORGE* off St. Catherines Point, whilst on passage Boston — Hull.
MOURINO (1)	1583 1027	255.0 33.2 23.3	Schlesinger Newcastle 1877	Sold 14.3.1896, to P. McGuffie & Co. Liverpool. Hulked at Kiel 1899.
OTRANTO	2353 1887	305.0 36.3 27.8	Earle's Hull 1877	Stranded on Fire Island 15.02.1896. Sold by auction 24.5.1896 at New York for $6,000 for scrapping at Long Island.

BOUGHT 1878 FROM BROWNLOW MARSDIN & CO.

NAME FORMER NAMES	GROSS NET	LENGTH BREADTH DEPTH	BUILDER PLACE YEAR	OTHER DETAILS
FALCON	441 270	174.1 24.1 14.1	Denny Dumbarton 1854	Bought 1878 from Brownlow Marsdin & Co. Scrapped 1894 by Wilson's.
FLAMINGO (1) x *LEOPARD*	849 550	223.1 28.9 16.5	Brownlow & Pearson Hull 1858	Bought 1878 from Brownlow Marsdin & Co. Renamed *FLAMINGO* 1879. Sold 28.9.1900, to Wm. Cory & Son, London. Hulked 1902.
LUMSDEN	1481 1213	250.7 34.1 18.3	Pearse Stockton 1869	Bought 1878 from Brownlow Marsdin & Co. Wrecked 16.7.1878, near Lemvig, Jutland. On passage Hull — St. Petersburg. All passengers and crew landed safely.
LIVORNO (1) x *MARSDIN*	1456 947	258.0 34.3 18.2	Humphry & Pearson Hull 1870	Bought 1878 from Brownlow Marsdin & Co. Renamed *LIVORNO* 1899. Sold 1.3.1901, T. B. Stott & Co. Liverpool. (Sambur Steamship Co.). Stranded 1.6.1907 at Walsoearne and subsequently scrapped.
PANTHER	912 590	235.2 27.7 14.2	Brownlow & Pearson Hull, 1861	Bought 1878 from Brownlow Marsdin & Co. Sold 3.1.1896 to W. E. Esplen & Co. Scrapped 1902.
PLATO (2) x *TIGER*	791 510	249.4 27.5 16.0	Brownlow & Pearson Hull 1857	Bought 1878 from Brownlow Marsdin & Co. Renamed *PLATO* 1889. Sold 13.11.1896 to Furness Withy. Scrapped in Holland 1902.

NAME FORMER NAMES	GROSS NET	LENGTH BREADTH DEPTH	BUILDER PLACE YEAR	OTHER DETAILS
ZEBRA	551 349	196.0 26.0 14.9	Brownlow & Pearson Hull, 1859	Bought 1878 from Brownlow Marsdin & Co. Sold 17.8.1894 to Furness Withy. Sold 29.10.1896, for scrapping.
RIALTO (1)	2229 1799	310.5 34.7 25.9	Earle's Hull 1878	Lost at sea by explosion and fire, whilst on passage Tyne — New York. Abandoned 5.3.1897.
SORRENTO (1)	2208 1798	301.0 34.7 26.0	Earle's Hull 1878	Sold 24.4.1895, to Furness Withy, Scrapped 1895.
BASSANO (1) x *ALTONA* x *ALFOUND*	1819 1183	280.0 35.0 24.5	Backhouse & Dickson Middlesbrough 1872	Built for R. C. Byrne, London as *ALFOUD*. Sold 1875, to W. Von Pusttau, Germany. Renamed *ALTONA*. 1877 stranded near Roker. Bought 29.5.1879 from the Deutsche Bank, Renamed *BASSANO*. Sold 30.12.1899, to Italian owners for scrapping at Genoa.
MARENGO (1)	2273 1509	299.5 37.2 25.5	Earle's Hull 1879	Sold 3.6.1901, to Sunderman & Zoon. For scrapping in Dordrecht.
SALERNO (1)	2059 1659	290.0 35.5 25.0	Earle's Hull 1879	Sold 19.7.1895 to N. Ricardo. For scrapping in Italy.
BORODINO (1)	1264 830	239.8 33.0 16.9	Earle's Hull 1880	Sold 26.2.1909, to F. Harris. For scrapping at Falmouth.
GITANO (1)	1243 820	240.1 33.0 16.9	Earle's Hull 1880	Sold 30.10.1909, to T. W. Ward. For scrapping at Preston.
SILVIO (1)	1193 787	239.0 32.1 16.8	Earle's Hull 1880	Sold 26.3.1912, to The Forth Shipbreaking Co. For scrapping at Boness.
GALILEO (1)	3008 1950	350.7 41.2 27.1	Earle's Hull 1881	Sold 26.10.1901 to Bruzzo Bross. For scrapping at Genoa.

ss. *LORENZO*
1893-1910
ENGINE: 2 cyl. Triple expansion
MADE BY: Wallsend Slipway Co. Newcastle.
POWER: 300 NHP
2 BOILERS 160lb per sq.in.
SPEED: 10 knots
SERVICE: India.
PASSENGERS: 10 — 1st Class.

ss. *HERO* 1895-1916
ENGINE: 3 cyl. Triple expansion
MADE BY: Earle's Shipbuilding & Eng. Co. Ltd. Hull.
POWER: 203 NHP
2 BOILERS 160lb per sq.in.
SPEED: 12½ knots
SERVICE: Continent.
PASSENGERS: 6 — 1st Class.

ss. *CASTELLO* 1896-1913

ENGINE:	3 cyl. Triple expansion
MADE BY:	W. Doxford, Sunderland.
POWER:	252 NHP
2 BOILERS	160lb per sq.in.
SPEED:	10 knots
SERVICE:	India.
PASSENGERS:	Nil.

ss. *ZERO (2)* 1896-1932

ENGINE:	3 cyl. Triple expansion
MADE BY:	Earle's Shipbuilding & Eng. Co. Ltd. Hull.
POWER:	161 NHP
2 BOILERS	190lb per sq.in.
SPEED:	12½ knots
SERVICE:	Copenhagen.
PASSENGERS:	14 — 1st Class. 197 — 3rd.

NAME FORMER NAMES	GROSS NET	LENGTH BREADTH DEPTH	BUILDER PLACE YEAR	OTHER DETAILS
ROMANO	2845 1876	330.0 39.0 27.6	Earle's Hull 1881	Lost 3.5.1884, in collision with NEVADA whilst on passage Hull — New York in position 43.N x 47.W.
ROMEO	1885 1157	275.0 34.6 19.9	Earle's Hull 1881	Sunk 3.3.1918, torpedoed by submarine U-102, 7 miles south of the Mull of Galloway. On passage to Liverpool in ballast, 29 crew including the Master were lost.
TOLEDO	1470 1149	260.0 34.0 17.9	Earle's Hull 1881	Sold 3.2.1908 to T. W. Ward. For scrapping.
CAIRO	1671 1085	270.8 34.1 18.3	Earle's Hull 1882	Sold 10.11.1903 to O. Winngren, Oskashamn. Sold 1914, renamed ALTE (Swedish). Sold 1921, to German owners. Scrapped 1924 as ALTE (German).
DRACO (1)	1713 1097	270.2 34.1 18.4	Earle's Hull 1882	Sold 17.1.1905 to J. Palmer, London. Posted missing Aug. 1908.
GRODNO (1)	1695 1104	269.9 34.1 18.4	Earle's Hull 1882	Sold 19.6.1911, to J. J. King, Garston. For scrapping.
JUNO (4)	1302 835	250.2 32.2 16.5	Earle's Hull 1882	Sold 16.10.1888, to The Tyne Steam Shipping Co. Newcastle. Detained at Hamburg 1914-1918 War. Returned 27.12.1918. Sold 1919, AFRA (Portuguese). Also renamed LECA, EL AMIGO and EDITH F. Scrapped 1935, as CECILIA (Nicaraguan).
KOVNO (1)	1708 1060	267.0 34.1 18.1	Earle's Hull 1882	Sold 12.3.1903 to I. Ingmansson, Salvesborg. Renamed SVEA. Sold 1918, Renamed TILIA (Swedish). Lost 3.2.1926 as MAITLAND (Swedish), after being in collision in the Thames estuary, 5 miles south of Cross Sand. On passage Oslo — Ridham Dock.
DEFIANCE (TUG) x CHARLEY	110 21	87.8 17.6 9.6	H. H. Price Neath Abbey 1862	Bought 28.2.1883, from J. Taylor Sunderland. Sold 10.9.1895, to North Shields owners. Scrapped March, 1904.
ROSARIO	1862 1222	275.3 34.3 19.2	Earle's Hull 1883	Sold 4.10.1905 to Nathan Mess., Shanghai. Renamed KIANGPING. Scrapped 1934.

NAME FORMER NAMES	GROSS NET	LENGTH BREADTH DEPTH	BUILDER PLACE YEAR	OTHER DETAILS
DYNAMO (1)	504 311	175.7 25.0 13.8	Earle's Hull 1884	Sold 1906, to Wilson's & North Eastern Railway Shipping Co. Sold 4.7.1912, to L. Brown, South Shields. Scrapped 1926, as *UNIONE* (Tunisian).
ELECTRO (1)	510 305	179.2 25.0 13.8	Earle's Hull 1884	Foundered 19.11.1893, 20 miles N.W. of Heligoland, whilst on passage Hull — Hamburg.
SALERNO (2) x *CHICAGO (1)* x *LINCOLN CITY*	2672 1683	301.0 40.0 22.6	W. Gray West Hartlepool 1884	Bought 20.11.1884 from Furness Withy. Renamed *CHICAGO* 1885. Renamed *SALERNO* 1898. Sold 14.12.1900, to W. Wilhelmsen, Tonsberg. Wrecked 30.6.1905, on Lichfield Shoal, Halifax N.S. On passage Cadiz — St. John N.B.
MARTELLO	3721 2417	370.0 43.1 28.4	Earle's Hull 1884	Sold 3.3.1910. to Adrien Merveille. For scrapping at Dunkirk.
MOSQUITO *(TUG)*	61 —	72.0 15.7 8.7	Earle's Hull 1884	Built for the use of Wilson vessels at Riga. Left Hull 29.6.1884. Under Russian Flag. Registered as owned by Helmsin & Grimm. But actually owned by Wilson's.
BUFFALO (1)	4427 2909	385.0 45.3 27.8	Palmer & Co. Newcastle 1885	Sold 4.11.1903, to Cerruti Bros. For scrapping at Genoa.
ELDORADO (2)	935 427	235.0 30.0 14.8	Earle's Hull 1885	Sold 11.2.1886, to the Greek Government, renamed *SFAKTIREA*, naval auxiliary. Sold 1906, renamed *MYKALI* (Greek) 1929, renamed *MYKALI TOGIA* (Greek). Scrapped in Italy 1933.
TORPEDO	487 300	150.3 25.1 13.0	Earle's Hull 1885	Sold 31.7.1905, to E. Levantis, Piraeus. Renamed *VYRON*. Changed to *BYRON* 1909. Sold 1912, renamed *SOUKHOUM* scrapped 1922.
ELDORADO (3)	1382 944	249.6 33.2 15.7	Earle's Hull 1886	Sold 16.9.1913, to J. Cashmore. For scrapping at Newport.
SANTIAGO	4188 2724	365.0 44.7 28.9	Raylton Dixon Middlesbrough 1886	Lost 1889, on fire North Atlantic. Abandoned 19.11.1889. On passage from New York — Hull.
THURSO (1) x *EASTELLA*	974 628	211.0 29.3 16.5	Blumer Sunderland 1871	Bought 6.4.1886 from Jackson, Beaumont & Co. Hull. Renamed *THURSO (1)*. Sold 6.12.1893, to Thompson Elliot, Sunderland. Posted missing since 10.2.1894 on passage Tyne-Hamburg.

ss. *ARGO* 1898-1932

ENGINE: 3 cyl. Triple expansion
MADE BY: Caledon Shipbuilding Co. Dundee.
POWER: 163 NHP
2 BOILERS 190lb per sq.in.
SPEED: 10½ knots
SERVICE: Continent.
PASSENGERS:
   8 — 1st Class.
   168 — 3rd.

ss. *ALEPPO* 1900-1929

ENGINE:
   3 cyl. Triple expansion
MADE BY:
   Furness, Westgarth & Co. Middlesbrough.
POWER:
   210 NHP
2 BOILERS
   165lb per sq.in.
SPEED:
   8½ knots
SERVICE:
   India.
PASSENGERS:
   2—1st Class.

ss. *SALMO (1)* 1900-1917

ENGINE:	3 cyl. Triple expansion
MADE BY:	Caledon Ship-building Co. Dundee.
POWER:	231 NHP
2 BOILERS	200lb per sq.in.
SPEED:	13½ knots
SERVICE:	Norway.
PASSENGERS:	58 — 1st Class.
	26 — 2nd.
	458 — 3rd.

ss. *DAGO (1)* 1902-1942

ENGINE:	3 cyl. Triple expansion
MADE BY:	Caledon Ship-building Co. Dundee.
POWER:	196 NHP
2 BOILERS	200lb per sq.in.
SPEED:	12 knots
SERVICE:	Copenhagen.
PASSENGERS:	12 — 1st Class.

NAME FORMER NAMES	GROSS NET	LENGTH BREADTH DEPTH	BUILDER PLACE YEAR	OTHER DETAILS
APOLLO (2)	3163 2066	330.4 41.2 29.0	Earle's Hull 1887	Posted missing April 1894, whilst on passage to New York — Antwerp. Left New York 11.2.1894.
COLORADO (1)	4235 2786	370.0 44.7 28.4	Earle's Hull 1887	Sold 13.11.1908, to J. Harris. For scrapping at Falmouth.
OHIO x *EGYPTIAN* *MONARCH*	3967 2557	360.0 43.1 24.8	A. McMillan & Son, Dumbarton 1881	Bought 2.8.1887, from Royal Exchange Shipping Co. London. Renamed *OHIO*. Sold 17.5.1904 to W. Mitchell. Wrecked 22.10.1904, at Ping Yang Inlet, Korea. On passage Muroran — Chinnampo.
ONTARIO x *LYDIAN* *MONARCH*	4036 2634	360.0 43.0 24.8	A. McMillan & Son, Dumbarton 1881	Bought 2.8.1887, from Royal Exchange Shipping Co. London. Renamed *ONTARIO*. Sold 4.9.1902, to J. King & Co. for scrapping at Garston.
PERSIAN *MONARCH*	3923 2569	360.0 43.1 22.6	A. McMillan & Son, Dumbarton 1880	Bought 12.8.1887, from Royal Exchange Shipping Co. London. Stranded 2.5.1894, E.S.E. of Moriches, New York on passage London — New York. Salved 4.5.1894, with severe machinery damage. Sold 5.1894 to J. I. J. Merrett, New York. Resold 7.1894, to R. C. Flint & Co. New York, who removed the engines and converted her into a 4 masted barque, at a cost of £23,000. Renamed *MAY* *FLINT* the vessel was the largest sailing ship on the U.S. Register, at the time. On 5.5.1889, caught fire at Kobe, Japan after arriving with a cargo of kerosene from Philadelphia, scuttled 6.5.1898. Refloated 11.5.1898. Sold 1899, renamed *PERSIAN MONARCH* (Barbados). Sold 1900, renamed *MAY FLINT* (San Francisco). Sold 1900, renamed *VIDETTE* (Hamburg). 9.9.1900, whilst on passage Nanaimo, Puget Sound — San Francisco, drifted onto the ram of the U.S. Battleship *IOWA* and sank. Salved and sold 21.9.1900 for scrapping.
JUMBO (TUG)	95 12	85.0 20.5 10.0	Head & Barnard Hull 1888	Sold 4.4.1911, to Grangemouth & Forth Towing Co. 1931, laid up for 11 months. Following a survey on 27.10.1936, considered uneconomic due to repair costs. Sold 28.10.1936 to N & G Burnham and subsequently scrapped in 1937.
VOLTURNO	2396 1566	297.0 40.1 19.0	Richardson Duck, Stockton 1888	Damaged by fire July 1912, at Marseilles. Sold to Wards for scrapping.

NAME FORMER NAMES	GROSS NET	LENGTH BREADTH DEPTH	BUILDER PLACE YEAR	OTHER DETAILS
CLIO (2)	2733 1778	300.0 40.7 21.1	Wm. Gray West Hartlepool 1889	Sold 11.11.1914, to The Admiralty for use as a block ship at Scapa flow.
DOURO	2442 1606	297.0 40.1 19.0	Richardson Duck, Stockton 1889	Sold 3.10.1929. to A. Stavuridis & B. A. Sardis, Piraeus. Renamed *KIMOLOS*. Scrapped 1933.
EBRO	2464 1618	296.7 40.1 19.0	Richardson Duck, Stockton 1889	Sold 21.12.1912, to D. Anghelatos, Piraeus. Renamed *OLYMPIA*. Sold 1916 Renamed *ALKYON* (Greek). Torpedoed 22.9.1917, in the Mediterranean.
HINDOO (2)	3720 2407	368.4 43.1 28.0	R. Stephenson & Co. Newcastle 1889	Sold 28.10.1904 to C. Andersen, Hamburg. Scrapped 1906 at Felixstowe.
IAGO (1)	2354 1572	295.1 38.1 20.0	Raylton Dixon Middlesbrough 1889	Sold 16.6.1908 to J. Harris for scrapping at Falmouth.
JUNO (5)	1073 644	215.1 30.4 14.9	Earle's Hull 1889	Sold 7.10.1899, to Bergen S.S. Co. Renamed *HERA*. Wrecked 17/18.3.1931, between Honningsvarg and Hammerfest, during storm. 6 people were lost — 56 saved.
KOLPINO (1)	2352 1553	295.0 39.0 19.3	R. Stephenson & Co. Newcastle 1889	Sold 25.3.1905, to Hiroumi Nisaburo, Uraga, Japan. Renamed *OMURO MARU*. Scrapped 1924.
POLO (1)	509 288	160.0 25.0 14.0	Earle's Hull 1889	Sold 23.9.1910, to Joaquim Maric Leite, Brazil. Renamed *VENEZA*. Scrapped 1913 in Brazil.
URBINO (2)	2429 1588	294.0 39.1 19.3	R. Thompson & Sons, Sunderland, 1889	Sold 19.11.1908, to J. Harris, for scrapping at Falmouth.
ARIOSTO (1)	2376 1545	300.4 38.0 20.0	Earle's Hull 1890	Sold 28.6.1910, to La Roda Hermanos, Valencia. Renamed *LUIS VIVES*. Torpedoed 11.9.1916, off Scilly Islands. On passage Valencia — Liverpool.
CONGO	2906 1892	307.0 41.4 20.7	Richardson Duck, Stockton 1890	Sold 7.8.1909, to J. Roussos & Sons, Greece. Renamed *NICOLAOS ROUSSOS*. Torpedoed 4.10.1917, in the Mediterranean. On passage Tyne — Spezia.

ss. *RONDA* 1903-1915

ENGINE:	3 cyl. Triple expansion
MADE BY:	Amos and Smith, Hull
POWER:	196 NHP
2 BOILERS	160lb per sq.in.
SPEED:	9 knots
SERVICE:	Baltic.
PASSENGERS:	Nil.

ss. *UNA* 1903-1909

ENGINE:	3 cyl. Triple expansion
MADE BY:	J. Scott & Co. Kinghorn.
POWER:	274 NHP
2 BOILERS	180lb per sq.in.
SPEED:	13 knots
SERVICE:	Copenhagen.
PASSENGERS:	58 — 1st Class.

ss. *IDAHO (3)* 1903-1929

ENGINE:	Quad 4 cyl.
MADE BY:	Earle's Ship-building & Eng. Co. Ltd. Hull.
POWER:	95 RHP
3 BOILERS	215lb per sq.in.
SPEED:	10 knots
SERVICE:	North America.
PASSENGERS:	4 — 1st Class.

ss. *CALYPSO (2)* 1904-1916

ENGINE:	3 cyl. Triple expansion
MADE BY:	Earle's Ship building & Eng. Co. Ltd. Hull.
POWER:	283 NHP
3 BOILERS	180lb per sq.in.
SPEED:	14 knots
SERVICE:	Norway.
PASSENGERS:	
	57 — 1st Class.
	44 — 2nd.
	863 — 3rd.

NAME FORMER NAMES	GROSS NET	LENGTH BREADTH DEPTH	BUILDER PLACE YEAR	OTHER DETAILS
MONTEBELLO (1)	1735 1115	276.0 35.0 15.6	Richardson Duck, Stockton 1890	Sold 28.6.1910, to Company Valenciana, Spain. Renamed *BARCELO*. Sold for scrapping 1929.
TASSO (2)	1328 936	250.0 32.0 14.8	Earle's Hull 1890	Sold 22.7.1911, to W. Morphy, Hull. Sold 1913, renamed *ELEFIS* (Greek). Foundered between Corsica — Elba, 25.12.1920. As *PHOTIOS* (Greek).
VOLO (1)	1289 841	260.2 32.0 16.4	Earle's Hull 1890	Sold 4.11.1924, to The Southampton Shipping Metal & Shingle Co. for scrapping.
FRANCISCO (1)	4788 2792	370.2 46.6 27.6	R. Stephenson & Co. Newcastle, 1891	Sold 28.10.1899, to French Line (C.G.T.) Renamed *BORDEAUX*. Torpedoed 7.9.1915, in the Bay of Biscay.
BRUNO	841 424	232.0 30.0 14.1	Earle's Hull 1892	Transferred 1906, to Wilson's & North Eastern Railway Company Sold 18.12.1909, to R. L. Newman, Victoria, B.C. Renamed *PRINCE ALBERT*. In 1935, Converted to oil burning Tug. Renamed *J. R. MORGAN* (Vancouver). Foundered 5.1950, at Vancouver.
ALECTO	3607 2341	346.0 43.1 19.1	Richardson Duck, Stockton 1893	Sold 24.8.1910, to T. Panaglos, Syria. Renamed *PANGALOS*. Sold 1915, renamed *MAR TERSO* (Italian). Torpedoed 27.5.1916, Mediterranean 39.08N 05.02E. On passage Newport — Savona.
FINLAND	1828 1170	271.1 35.1 18.6	Earle's Hull 1884	Bought 27.6.1893, from G. R. Sanderson, Hull. Lost 15.12.1917, in collision with *POLE STAR*, 10 miles N.E. of Auskerry, Orkney's.
HORATIO (1) x *HORSLEY TOWER*	3212 2078	331.0 40.2 19.1	Edward's SB.Co. Newcastle 1892	Bought 24.11.1893, from F. Strumore, London. Renamed *HORATIO*. Sold 5.5.1895, to Booth Line. Sold 1911, to T. Salvesen of Leith. Converted into a floating whale factory ship. Destroyed by fire 11.3.1916, at Leith Harbour South Shetlands. Sank outside harbour under tow after cargo of 11,000 barrels of oil caught fire. A fate which befell several of this type of vessel.
LORENZO x *LANSDOWNE TOWER*	3191 2031	331.5 40.5 19.2	W. Dobson & Co Newcastle 1890	Bought 28.11.1893, from F. Strumore, London. Renamed *LORENZO*. Sold 2.5.1910, to J. A. Mango, Piraeus. Renamed *MARIA MANGO*. Posted missing 1911.

NAME FORMER NAMES	GROSS NET	LENGTH BREADTH DEPTH	BUILDER PLACE YEAR	OTHER DETAILS
MURILLO	2419 1557	301.0 39.5 19.9	J. Priestman & Co., Sunderland 1893	Sold 19.5.1914, to M. J. Mango, Piraeus. Renamed *EPTALOFOS*. Wrecked 23.5.1923, on Isle de Re whilst on passage Huelva — La Pallice.
CORSO	895 410	234.0 31.0 14.4	Priestman Sunderland 1893	Lost 16.11.1898, in collision with the British vessel ss. *GERMAN* in dense fog on the River Elbe, near Glameyers Stack. On passage Hamburg — Hull. All the crew of the *CORSO* were rescued by lifeboat from the ss. *GERMAN*.
HETTY	532 334	165.7 24.7 13.8	Raylton Dixon Middlesbrough 1894	Bought 15.5.1894, from T. F. Bell & Co. Hull. Lost 26.7.1894, in collision off Whitby.
MIKADO	3557 2306	346.0 43.1 19.1	Richardson Duck, Stockton 1894	Sold 20.6.1911, to P. Liakakis, Piraeus. Renamed *KIOS* . Scrapped 1925.
PRESTO (1) (TUG) x *TRIUMPH*	155 27	107.0 19.6 10.0	J. Eltringham South Shields 1893	Bought 17.8.1894, renamed *PRESTO (1)*. Sold 14.11.1923, to C. Duncan & Sons, Middlesbrough. Renamed *BEATTIE DUNCAN*. Sold 1928, to Aberdeen Steam Tug Co. Ltd. Scrapped 1933, at Aberdeen.
CICERO (1)	1834 1185	270.0 38.1 19.1	Earle's Hull 1895	Scuttled 10.4.1918, to avoid capture, at Petrograd (Baltic).
HERO (3)	775 331	216.5 30.0 13.6	Earle's Hull 1895	Transferred 1906, to Wilson's & North Eastern Railway Shipping Co. Sold 1916, to General Steam Navigation Co. Sold 1923, to Ellerman Line. Sold 25.1.1929, to General Steam Navigation Co. Scrapped 1933.
SCIPIO	1735 1118	270.2 38.1 19.0	Furness, Withy & Co. West Hartlepool 1895	Sold 3.4.1927, to J. Siering & Co. Riga. Renamed *LIDUMS*. Scrapped 1934, at Copenhagen.
TOKIO	3827 2481	363.0 45.5 27.2	Richardson Duck, Stockton 1895	Sold 13.12.1911, to Atlantic Whaling Co. Norway. Renamed POLYNESIA. Torpedoed 10.9.1916, 50 miles S.W. of the Scilly Isles. On passage New York — London.
VASCO (1)	1914 1216	280.0 40.0 19.2	Furness, Withy & Co. West Hartlepool 1895	Sank 16.11.1916, struck a mine laid by submarine UC-16. 10 miles W by S of Beachy Head. On passage Hull — Naples. 17 crew including the Master were lost.

ss. *OSLO* 1906-1917

ENGINE:	3 cyl. Triple expansion
MADE BY:	Earle's Ship-building & Eng. Co. Ltd. Hull.
POWER:	233 NHP
2 BOILERS	180lb per sq.in.
SPEED:	13 knots
SERVICE:	Norway.
PASSENGERS:	62 — 1st Class.
	36 — 2nd.
	781 — 3rd.

ss. *BUFFALO (2)* 1907-1917

ENGINE:	Quad 4 cyl.
MADE BY:	Earle's Ship-building & Eng. Co. Ltd. Hull.
POWER:	262 NHP
2 BOILERS	215lb per sq.in.
SPEED:	11 knots
SERVICE:	North America.
PASSENGERS:	Nil.

ss. _YORK_ 1907-1937

ENGINE:	3 cyl. Triple expansion
MADE BY:	Caledon Ship-building Co. Dundee.
POWER:	195 NHP
2 BOILERS	180lb per sq.in.
SPEED:	14½ knots
SERVICE:	Hamburg.
PASSENGERS:	12 — 1st Class. 1484 — 3rd.

ss. _HIDALGO (2)_ 1908-1917

ENGINE:	3 cyl. Triple expansion
MADE BY:	Richardson, Westgarth Co. Sunderland.
POWER:	372 NHP
3 BOILERS	180lb per sq.in.
SPEED:	9½ knots
SERVICE:	Mediter-ranean, Black Sea.
PASSENGERS:	Nil.

NAME FORMER NAMES	GROSS NET	LENGTH BREADTH DEPTH	BUILDER PLACE YEAR	OTHER DETAILS
CASTELLO	3635 2339	351.0 46.0 25.0	W. Doxford & Sons, Sunderland, 1896	Sold 27.6.1913, to D. Anghelatos, Greece. Renamed *GRIGORIOS ANGHELATOS*. Torpedoed 5.12.1916, in the Mediterranean. On passage Barcelona — London.
DIDO (2)	4769 3127	400.7 48.0 28.2	Earle's Hull 1896	Sank 26.2.1916, struck a mine laid by submarine UC-7, 4 miles N.N.E. Spurn Lightship. On passage Middlesbrough — Hull — Bombay. 28 Crewmen lost, 3 survivors picked up by Belgian steamer *MARTHA*.
HORATIO (2)	3197 2081	330.0 43.0 26.7	Furness, Withy & Co. West Hartlepool 1896	Wrecked 21.4.1904, at Muros Bay, near Cape Villano. On passage Odessa — Hull.
IDAHO (1) x *MEGANTIC*	5532 3614	450.0 49.1 30.9	Stephenson & Sons Glasgow 1896	Bought from builders as *MEGANTIC*. Transferred 15.10.1896, to Wilson, Furness, Leyland Line. Renamed *LONDONIAN*. Abandoned Nov. 1898, North Atlantic. 45 crew rescued by the liner *VEDAMORE,* 8 more rescued by *MARIA RICKMERS*. 17 persons lost.
SPERO (1)	1132 724	250.5 30.1 15.6	A. McMillan & Son, Dumbarton 1896	2.11.1916, Captured by submarine U-69, 95 miles W.S.W. of Helliso Light House, Norway, and sunk by torpedo On passage Bergen — Hull.
ZERO (2)	1143 735	249.8 30.0 15.7	Earle's Hull 1896	Sold 1932, to G. & W. Brunton. for scrapping at Grangemouth. Left Hull 6.10.1932.
OTHELLO (2)	5059 3327	420.0 48.2 28.8	Earle's Hull 1897	Sold 26.7.1926, to Zeevaart Maats S. A. Ghent. Renamed *SCHELDEPAS*. Wrecked 14.3.1929, at Plane Island. On passage Antwerp — Shanghai.
ARGO (2)	1102 605	220.0 32.0 14.5	Caledon SB Co. Dundee 1898	Sold 28.12.1932, to Gt. Grimsby Marine Scrap Ltd. for scrapping.
CHICAGO (2)	6438 4315	475.5 52.3 23.2	Furness, Withy & Co. West Hartlepool 1898	Transferred, 7.2.1899, to Wilson, Furness, Leyland Line. Renamed *ETONIAN*. Torpedoed 23.3.1918, 34 miles S by E from Old head of Kinsdale.

NAME FORMER NAMES	GROSS NET	LENGTH BREADTH DEPTH	BUILDER PLACE YEAR	OTHER DETAILS
CLEOPATRA	6889	482.0 52.3 31.5	Earle's Hull 1898	Sold 2.8.1898, to Atlantic Transport Co., London. Renamed *MOHEGAN*. On 13.10.1898, the *MOHEGAN* sailed from Tilbury with 53 passengers, 97 crew and 7 cattlemen. On 14.10.1898 as the vessel past Prawle Point she signalled her position. The coastguard at Coverack realising the *MOHEGAN* was too close to the Manacle rocks tried to alert her by firing rockets, but to no avail, at 6.50 pm she struck the Outer Manacle rocks. In minutes the *MOHEGAN* was three parts under water, finally sinking in 10 minutes. 106 people lost their lives in the disaster.
IDAHO (2)	6210 3802	460.0 50.1 31.6	C.S. Swan Hunter. Newcastle, 1898	Sold 16.1.1902, to Cia. Sud Americana de Nav. Valparaiso, Chile. Renamed *RANCAGUA*. Sold 1930, by Chilean Gov. for scrapping.
OTTO (2)	836 272	225.0 32.1 12.0	Caledon SB Co. Dundee 1898	Transferred 1906, to Wilson's & North Eastern Railway Shipping Co. Sold 1936, for scrapping.
SAPPHO (2) *CASTRO (3) x MICHAIL	1318 804	266.0 33.6 15.4	Caledon SB Co. Dundee 1898	Sold 26.4.1901, to Helmsing & Grimm, Riga. Renamed *MICHAIL* 1920, returned to Ellerman's Wilson Line. renamed *CASTRO*. Sold 1923, to Baltic S.S. Co. Leningrad. Renamed *GERTZEN*. Wrecked 1935.
TRURO (1)	836 272	225.0 32.1 12.0	Caledon SB. Co. Dundee 1898	6.6.1915, Captured by submarine U-39, 85 miles E.N.E. of St. Abbs Head and sunk by torpedo. On passage Christiania — Grimsby. All crew saved.
ZAIMIS	332 148	155.7 22.6 9.8	Richardson Duck, Stockton 1860	Bought 11.11.1898, from Rawson & Robinson, Hull. Sold 15.9.1899, to Paton & Hendry Glasgow. Sold 1909, renamed *TACUARY* (Uruguay). Scrapped 1912.
CASTRO (1) *SERGEI	1150 830	262.5 33.5 15.8	Earle's Hull 1899	Sold 7.5.1901, to Helmsing & Grim, Wilson Line agents, Riga. Renamed *SERGEI*. 1920, returned to Ellerman's Wilson Line. Lost 19.8.1923, in collision with *JUNO*, in the River Humber. All crew saved.
CITO (1)	860 347	219.1 30.1 16.5	Earle's Hull 1899	Transferred 1906 to Wilson & North Eastern Railway Shipping Co. Sunk 17.5.1917 by German M.T.B. Destroyer 20 miles N.E. of the North Hinder Lightvessel. On passage Hull — Rotterdam. 11 crew including the Master were lost.

ss. *ESKIMO* 1910-1921

ENGINE:	Quad 8 cyl.
MADE BY:	Earle's Ship-building & Eng. Co. Ltd. Hull.
POWER:	373 NHP
4 BOILERS	215lb per sq.in.
SPEED:	17 knots
SERVICE:	Norway.
PASSENGERS:	109 — 1st Class.
	39 — 2nd.
	284 — open 3rd.
	136 — in rooms.

ss. *FRANCISCO (2)* 1910-1935

ENGINE:	3 cyl. Triple expansion
MADE BY:	Earle's Shipbuilding & Eng. Co. Ltd. Hull.
POWER:	424 NHP
3 BOILERS	180lb per sq.in.
SPEED:	11 knots
SERVICE:	North America.
PASSENGERS:	Nil.

ss. *BAYARDO* 1911-1912

ENGINE:	3 cyl. Triple expansion
MADE BY:	Earle's Ship building & Eng. Co. Ltd. Hull.
POWER:	288 NHP
3 BOILERS	180lb per sq.in.
SPEED:	15 knots
SERVICE:	Norway.
PASSENGERS:	39 — 1st Class.
	54 — 2nd.
	568 — 3rd.

ss. *BORODINO (2)* 1911-1939

ENGINE:	3 cyl. Triple expansion
MADE BY:	Earle's Shipbuilding & Eng. Co. Ltd. Hull.
POWER:	233 NHP
2 BOILERS	200lb per sq.in.
SPEED:	12 knots
SERVICE:	Mediterranean.
PASSENGERS:	27 — 1st Class.

*The s.s. **North Sea** built by C. and W. J. Earle, 1855 and wrecked near Jutland, 1859, drawn and lithographed by S. H. Wilson, printed by W. Monkhouse, York.* (Town Docks Museum, Hull).

*The s.s. **Atlantic** built by C. and W. J. Earle, 1857, and sold to Moss of Liverpool, 1860; a watercolour by S. H. Wilson.* (Town Docks Museum, Hull).

*The s.s. **Oder** (left) built 1861 and lost in the North Sea 1875; the s.s. **Ouse** (right) built 1862 and wrecked off Jutland 1867. Both vessels constructed by C. and W. J. Earle; a watercolour by S. H. Wilson. (Town Docks Museum, Hull).*

*The s.s. **Calypso** built by C. and W. J. Earle, 1865, sold in 1902 for scrap. She flies the Imperial Russian tricolour and the Wilson Line house flag; an oil painting signed John Loos, Antwerp, 1871. (Town Docks Museum, Hull).*

The s.s. **Othello**, a steamer in the Indian and N. American trades, here flying the U.S. courtesy flag and working the New York route which she inaugurated for Wilsons. Built in 1872 by C. and W. J. Earle and sold in 1895 for scrap. An oil painting signed Antonio Jacobsen 157, 8th Ave. NY, 1879. (Town Docks Museum, Hull).

The twin-funnelled s.s. **Buffalo**, built 1885 by Palmer's of Newcastle and sold in 1903 for scrap. An oil painting of a regular transatlantic steamer, signed Antonio Jacobsen, 1886, 705 Palisade Avenue, W. Hoboken, N.Y. (Town Docks Museum, Hull).

*Tinted general arrangement plan of the s.s. **Colorado** built 1887 by C. and W. J. Earle, sold for scrap in 1908. Drawn on paper and signed Alex. More, 26.9.88. (Town Docks Museum, Hull).*

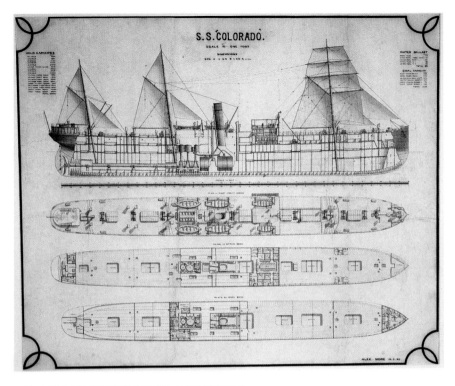

*The s.s. **Marengo**, built 1879 by C. and W. J. Earle and sold 1901 for scrap. Here shown outward bound from New York for Newcastle and Hull in the command of Capt. Whitton. On 24 December 1893 in heavy snow squalls a boat was put down to rescue 10 hands from the **Pilot Cutter No.20** of New York. An oil painting by Conrad Freitag, Brooklyn, N.W. (Town Docks Museum, Hull).*

*The s.s. **Syria** built 1859 by Raylton, Dixon of Middlesbrough for Bailey and Leetham. Acquired by Wilsons 1903 and seen here in the Bay of Naples flying an Italian courtesy flag and the Wilson house flag, a white burgee with a red ball; sold for scrap in 1912. An oil painting, unsigned. (Town Docks Museum, Hull).*

*The s.s. **Cito** built by C. and W. J. Earle in 1899 and transferred in 1906 to the Wilson and North Eastern Shipping Co. Here carrying a Belgian courtesy flag and the square WNER house flag, a variant of the Wilson one with three railway company shields superimposed on the red ball. (Town Docks Museum, Hull).*

The R.M.S. **Eskimo** *built in 1910 by Earles Shipbuilding and Engineering Co, the pride of the prewar fleet; sold to French owners in 1921 and scrapped in 1929. A gouache study for a poster.*
(Town Docks Museum, Hull).

The m.v. **Salerno** *built 1963 by Henry Robb of Leith, first of the S-class vessels, and transferred to Ellerman City Lines in 1973; general cargo vessel with special facilities for containers and palletised cargo. Gouache drawing by J. Cobb.*
(Town Docks Museum, Hull).

NAME FORMER NAMES	GROSS NET	LENGTH BREADTH DEPTH	BUILDER PLACE YEAR	OTHER DETAILS
HYDRO (1)	1392 855	262.0 33.5 15.8	Earle's Hull 1899	Sold 24.4.1901, to Rigaer Schnell Dampfer Ges. Riga, Latvia. (Helmsing & Grimm). Renamed *WELIKIJ KNIAZ ALEXANDER MICHAILOWITSCH*. Returned to Wilson's ownership in 1920. 1924, Renamed *ROSCHAL* (U.S.S.R. government fleet). Scrapped 1960.
SALVO (TUG)	267 24	121.0 24.1 11.4	J. Eltringham South Shields 1899	Sold 30.4.1901, to the Admiralty. Sold 1922, to W. MacNab. Unlisted from 1926, probably scrapped.
ALEPPO	3870 2537	340.0 47.2 27.3	Stephenson Newcastle 1900	Sold 24.7.1929, to A. Gioffrida, Catonia, Italy. Renamed *APOLLO*. Scrapped in Italy 1933.
CLARO	2187 1395	300.0 42.2 28.8	Earle's Hull 1900	Sold 29.8.1926, to A. V. Sperling, Riga. Renamed *TRANSTEVE* Sold 1927, renamed *VAIDAVA* (Latvian). Stranded 27.5.1934, near Llanelly salved and sold for scrapping.
COLENSO	3861 2532	340.0 47.2 20.1	Stephenson Newcastle 1900	30.11.1915, captured by submarine U-33, 95 miles E.S.E. of Malta, and sunk by gunfire. On passage Alexandria — Hull. 1 crewman lost.
CONSUELLO (1)	6025 3960	461.5 52.1 31.1	C. S. Swan Hunter, Newcastle, 1900	Sold 21.5.1908, to Cairn Line Steamships Ltd. Renamed *CAIRNRONA*. Sold 1911, Renamed *ALBANIA* (Cunard Line). Sold 1912, Renamed *POLERIC* (Bank Line). Sold 1927 to Japanese owners. Scrapped 1929 in Japan.
JUNO (6)	905 373	235.0 32.0 15.0	Earle's Hull 1900	Transferred 1906, to Wilson's & North Eastern Railway Shipping Co. Sold 22.4.1926, for scrapping at Preston.
MOROCCO	3783 2476	340.0 47.2 19.5	Furness, Withy & Co. West Hartlepool 1900	Sold 3.7.1930, to Cia. Colonial de Nav. Renamed *PUNGUE*. For use as a hulk off Beira, Portuguese South Africa. Scrapped in 1961.
SALMO (1)	1722 1095	268.0 35.2 16.2	Caledon SB Co. Dundee 1900	Sunk 7.4.1917, torpedoed by sumbarine U-60, 210 miles N.W. of Fastnet. 52.30 N 14.40 W. On passage Oporto — Liverpool. 2 crewmen were lost.
TORONTO	6035 3949	456.0 52.2 31.1	Wm. Gray West Hartlepool 1900	Sold 4.4.1923, to Hendrich & Auracht. For scrapping in Holland.

NAME FORMER NAMES	GROSS NET	LENGTH BREADTH DEPTH	BUILDER PLACE YEAR	OTHER DETAILS
LIDO	977 602	225.4 30.1 16.8	Murdoch & Murray, Pt Glasgow 1901	Bought 16.11.1901, from Swedish owners. Sold 18.6.1906, to G. Focas, Argostoli, Greece. Renamed *HELEN*. Sold 1915, renamed *ELENA* (Rumanian). Sold 1926, renamed *MARTIS* (Greek). Sold 1929, renamed *AGHIOS NICOLAOS* (Greek). Scrapped 1930, at Spezia.
PLATO (3) (TUG)	135 —	90.0 22.1 9.5	Cook, Welton & Gemmell, Hull 1901	Sold 10.3.1939, to J. A. White, Leith. Renamed *PLETO*. Scrapped 1964.
DAGO (1)	1757 1057	296.0 37.2 17.4	Caledon SB Co. Dundee 1902	Sunk 15.3.1942, by bombs during air attack north of Lisbon. 39.19 N 09.26 W. On passage Lisbon — Oporto. All 37 crew saved.
NOVO	1655 1037	280.4 37.1 17.6	Stephenson Newcastle 1902	Sold 13.3.1928, to T. Ward for scrapping at Inverkeithing.
RUNO (1)	1654 1044	280.0 37.2 17.4	Caledon SB Co. Dundee 1902	Sunk 5.9.1914, mined 22 miles E by N of the Tyne. On passage Hull — Archangel, with a large number of passengers. 29 persons were lost. It was later proved that the ship had deviated from her assigned route laid down by the Admiralty and had strayed into a known minefield.

THE VESSELS OF BAILEY & LEETHAM, FLEET ACQUIRED 1903

NAME FORMER NAMES	GROSS NET	LENGTH BREADTH DEPTH	BUILDER PLACE YEAR	OTHER DETAILS
ARGYLE	1185 767	241.6 30.9 15.8	Gilbert & Cooper, Hull 1872	Sold 10.9.1914, to the Admiralty for use as a blockship at Scapa flow.
AUSTRIA	2211 1396	284.0 39.1 18.2	Austin & Sons Sunderland 1890	Sold 15.7.1912, to Antwerpshe Zeevaart Maats, Renamed *ADUATIEK*. Mined 12.3.1916, in the North Sea.
BONA x *HIGHLAND PRINCE*	1581 934	240.0 36.1 16.9	Short Bros. Sunderland 1883	Sold 17.1.1905, to N. Kunstmann, Stettin. Renamed *TUETONIA*. Scrapped 1934.
DELTA	1109 552	225.4 34.2 15.2	J. Scott & Co. Kinghorn 1900	Sold 26.4.1904, to S. Hough, Liverpool. Renamed *ANNIE HOUGH*. Sold 1917, renamed *LANCASHIRE COAST*, (British). Sold 1919, renamed *ARWYCO* (British). Sold 1934, renamed *CORISCO* (Honduras). Sold 1941, renamed *CORINTO* (Cuban). Scrapped in 1949.

ss. *SERBINO* 1912-1915

ENGINE:	3 cyl. Triple expansion
MADE BY:	Dunlop, Bremner & Co. Pt. Glasgow.
POWER:	249 NHP
2 BOILERS	180lb per sq.in.
SPEED:	10½ knots
SERVICE:	Russia, Baltic.
PASSENGERS:	8 — 1st Class.

ss. *CARLO (1)* 1913-1917

ENGINE:	3 cyl. Triple expansion
MADE BY:	Clyde Ship-building & Eng. Co. Pt. Glasgow.
POWER:	185 NHP
2 BOILERS	180lb per sq.in.
SPEED:	10½ knots
SERVICE:	Mediter-ranean, Black Sea.
PASSENGERS:	Nil.

ss. _SMOLENSK_ 1916-1929

ENGINE:	3 cyl. Triple expansion
MADE BY:	N. Doxford & Sons Ltd. Sunderland.
POWER:	270 NHP
3 BOILERS	200lb per sq.in.
SPEED:	10½ knots
SERVICE:	Lower Baltic.
PASSENGERS:	10 — 1st Class
	76 — 2nd.
	578 — open 3rd.
	616 — in rooms.

ss. _THURSO (3)_ 1919-1942

ENGINE:	3 cyl. Triple expansion
MADE BY:	Richard, Westgarth & Co. Ltd. Sunderland.
POWER:	266 NHP
2 BOILERS	180lb per sq.in.
SPEED:	10 knots
SERVICE:	Mediterranean.
PASSENGERS:	Nil.

NAME FORMER NAMES	GROSS NET	LENGTH BREADTH DEPTH	BUILDER PLACE YEAR	OTHER DETAILS
ENVOY	1353 881	253.8 31.9 18.0	Gilbert & Cooper, Hull 1872	Foundered 8.11.1911, in the North Sea. Whilst on passage Hull — Stockholm.
ESPERANZA	789 424	220.0 28.6 15.6	J. G. Lawrie Glasgow 1871	Sold 14.10.1904, to Bells Asia Minor Co. Liverpool. Sold 1917, renamed *LEBDA* (Italian). Scrapped in 1917.
ESSEX	1219 780	238.0 31.7 17.0	Humphry & Pearson, Hull 1869	Sold 28.5.1909, to Adrien Merveille, for scrapping at Dunkirk.
FAIRY	659 419	195.2 26.4 15.3	Earle's Hull 1868	Sold 22.10.1910, to R. White & Sons, Widnes, for scrapping.
GENOA x *CENTURIAN*	1942 1233	276.5 38.1 16.2	Bloomer & Co. Sunderland 1890	Posted missing Jan. 1912. Whilst on passage Blyth — Riga. Lost in heavy weather.
JAFFA	1594 1025	260.1 35.2 16.4	J. Scott Kinghorn 1897	Sunk 2.2.1918, torpedoed by submarine UB-30, 3 miles E by S of Owers light vessel. On passage Boulogne — Southampton. 10 crew were lost.
KOTKA	1695 1099	260.0 36.2 18.5	M.S. Edward & Son, Newcastle 1884	Sold 19.7.1922, to Rederi A/G Estria, Norrkoping. Renamed *ESTER*. Sold 1931, renamed *VIKVALL* (Swedish). Sold 1935, renamed *MARY* (Swedish). Sold 1943, renamed *UTKLIPPAN 11* (Swedish). Wrecked, December 1949.
LORNE	1186 733	241.7 30.9 15.8	Gilbert & Cooper Hull, 1873	Sold 21.10.1914, to the Admiralty for use as a blockship at Scapa flow.
NARVA	1889 1234	275.2 35.4 19.1	Earle's Hull 1883	Sold 19.1.1926, to A. Alfino & Figli, Catania. Scrapped 1935, at Genoa.
ORIA	2167 1318	280.5 38.9 18.3	Thompson & Sons Sunderland 1880	Sold 5.5.1906, to J. Johanson & Co. Lysaker, Norway. Renamed *THORSDAL* Torpedoed 24.7.1917, west of Scotland. On passage Chatham, NFL. — Ardrossan.

NAME FORMER NAMES	GROSS NET	LENGTH BREADTH DEPTH	BUILDER PLACE YEAR	OTHER DETAILS
OXFORD	1282 802	243.6 38.9 17.1	Humphry & Pearson, Hull 1870	Badly damaged 22.4.1909, in collision with s.s. *EDITH* in Oslofjord. Subsequently sold for scrapping.
PERA	1150 623	225.0 34.0 14.4	Mackie & Thompson Glasgow, 1899	Sold 11.4.1904, to Salveson & Co. Sold 1907, to Schliewlensky & Ziegler Hamburg. Sold 1910, renamed *HAVEL* (German). Lost 7.1.1911, off Norfolk in collision with ss. *AXWELL*. On passage Santader — Stockholm.
RONDA x *RYDAL HOLME*	1941 1226	274.0 36..6 19.0	Bloomer & Co. Sunderland 1889	Sold 28.1.1915, to the Admiralty for use as a blockship at Scapa flow.
SULTAN	1041 661	239.2 31.4 14.7	Earle's Hull 1867	Sold 12.6.1914, to G. Longueville, Dunkirk. Renamed *QUANDMEME*. Scrapped in 1923.
SULTANA	1920 1207	265.0 36.1 23.0	Blyth SB Co. Blyth 1888	Sold 24.2.1905, to K. Yamamoto. Kobe. Renamed *MISHIMA MARU*. Scrapped 1931.
SYRIA	2239 1430	277.0 38.2 19.2	Raylton Dixon & Co. Middlesbrough 1889	Sold 18.1.1912, to Otto Banck, Helsinborg. Renamed *YRSA*. Sold 1916, renamed *MAGNUS BAY* (Swedish). Sold 1918, renamed *ERIKSHOLM* (Swedish). Sold 1919, renamed *SMYRNA* (Swedish). Sold 1924, renamed *PRESTONIC* (Swedish). Wrecked 9.11.1940 on Borkum as *MINERVA* (Finnish).
UNA	1407 769	237.2 34.2 16.8	J. Scott & Co Kinghorn 1899	Sold 4.12.1909, to Cia Valenciana. Spain. Renamed *VICENTE LA RODA*. Sunk 3.5.1938 at Palamos during the Spanish Civil War. Salved 1945, rebuilt as *JUAN ILLUECA* Wrecked 3.6.1960, at Cape Penas. On passage Bordeaux — Gijon.
WILLIAM BAILEY	1836 1215	275.3 34.3 18.9	Earle's Hull 1883	Stranded 10.3.1909, at Fasterbo. Subsequently scrapped at Malmo.
ZARA	1331 706	257.0 35.2 16.5	W. Hamilton & Co. Pt. Glasgow 1897	Sunk 13.4.1917, torpedoed by submarine U-30, 90 miles SW of Helliso Island, Norway. On passage London — Trondheim. 27 crew were lost.

ss. *URBINO (4)* 1919-1954

ENGINE:	3 cyl. Triple expansion
MADE BY:	Earle's Ship-building & Eng. Co. Ltd. Hull.
POWER:	369 NHP
3 BOILERS	180lb per sq.in.
SPEED:	11 knots
SERVICE:	North America.
PASSENGERS:	Nil.

ss. *CALYPSO (3)* 1920-1936

ENGINE:	3 cyl. Triple expansion
MADE BY:	T. Richardson & Sons, Hartlepool.
POWER:	432 NHP
3 BOILERS	180lb per sq.in.
SPEED:	12 knots
SERVICE:	Scandinavia, Lower Baltic.
PASSENGERS:	60 — 1st Class.
	20 — 2nd.
	60 — 3rd.

ss. *ORLANDO (2)* 1920-1932

ENGINE:	3 cyl. Triple expansion
MADE BY:	Hall, Russell & Co. Ltd. Aberdeen.
POWER:	525 NHP
6 BOILERS	180lb per sq.in.
SPEED:	13½ knots
SERVICE:	Scandinavia, Lower Baltic.
PASSENGERS:	76 — 1st Class. 620 — 3rd.

ss. *GITANO (3)* 1921-1955

ENGINE:	2 steam reduction geared turbines.
MADE BY:	British Westinghouse Elect, Manchester.
POWER:	1620 SHP
2 BOILERS	225lb per sq.in.
SPEED:	10½ knots
SERVICE:	North America.
PASSENGERS:	Nil.

Photograph courtesy of Fotoflite.

NAME FORMER NAMES	GROSS NET	LENGTH BREADTH DEPTH	BUILDER PLACE YEAR	OTHER DETAILS
IDAHO (3)	4887 3093	400.3 50.3 29.3	Earle's Hull 1903	Stranded 7.1.1929, near Aberdeen. On passage Hull — New York. Salved 16.7.1929. Sold to McLaren & Co. for scrapping at Pt. Glasgow.
SAPPHO (3)	1693 1046	282.0 40.0 18.5	Earle's Hull 1903	Abandoned 24.12.1915, whilst trapped in ice near Archangel. 20 crew perished trying to reach safety. 3 were saved. *SAPPHO* foundered 14.5.1916, whilst adrift in the Arctic ice fields.
CALYPSO (2)	2962 1718	309.6 42.7 23.9	Earle's Hull 1904	Taken up by the Admiralty in Nov. 1914, renamed H.M.S. *CALYX*, (M.86) 10th Cruiser Sqdn. Guns: eight 4.7″ and two 3 pounder guns. Returned to Wilson Line 26.6.1915. Sunk 10.7.1916, torpedoed by submarine U-53, in the Skagerrak off Lindesnes. On passage London — Kristiansand. 30 Crew including the Master were lost.
TORO	3066 1951	330.0 48.3 22.5	Earle's Hull 1904	Sunk 12.4.1917, torpedoed by submarine U-55, 200 miles W.N.W. of Ushant. 48.30 N 10.00 W. On passage Alexandria — Hull. The Master and the gunner were taken prisoner aboard the submarine. 14 crew were lost.
TYCHO	3216 2029	335.0 47.0 22.9	Earle's Hull 1904	Sunk 20.5.1917, torpedoed by submarine UB-40, 16 miles west of Beachy Head. On passage Bombay — Hull. 15 crew including the Master were lost.
HINDOO (3)	4915 3156	398.0 50.2 29.4	Earle's Hull 1905	Sold 2.10.1924, Margarita Macris, London. Renamed *ANASTASIA*. Sold 1926, renamed *ELISE SCHULTE* (German). Wrecked 25.12.1926, Norwegian Coast.
VIGO	3252 2020	336.0 48.3 22.8	Earle's Hull 1905	Sold 19.1.1927 to A. Giufrid, Catania. Renamed *ARCANGELO*. Sold 1933, renamed *INSPECTOR BENEDETTI* (Argentinian). Sold 1942, renamed *WANGO* (Portuguese). Sold 1949, renamed *CAPETAN LEFTERES* (Panamanian). Scrapped 1953 in Japan.
FIDO (2)	602 267	178.0 29.6 16.1	Earle's Hull 1906	Sold 8.6.1922, to H. Poole & Co. London. Renamed *POOLMINA*. Sold 1931, renamed *WEXFORDIAN*. Sold 1933, renamed *LADY CAVAN*. 1938, renamed *CAVAN*. Sold 1939, renamed *MARIOS* (Greek). Sunk 4.1941, War loss.
KOLPINO (2)	2098 1189	300.0 41.1 18.4	Earle's Hull 1906	Sold 4.4.1929, to Polish — British Shipping Co. Gdynia. Renamed *REWA*. Scrapped 1934, in Germany.

NAME FORMER NAMES	GROSS NET	LENGTH BREADTH DEPTH	BUILDER PLACE YEAR	OTHER DETAILS
MOURINO (2)	1819 947	300.0 41.5 18.4	Earle's Hull 1906	Sold 14.9.1939, to the Admiralty for use as ammunition hulk. Scrapped by Ward's at Briton Ferry 9.2.1951
OSLO	2296 1427	290.0 39.1 25.3	Earle's Hull 1906	Sunk 21.8.1917, torpedoed by submarine U-87, 15 miles E by N from the Outer Skerries of the Shetland Islands. On passage Trondheim — Liverpool. 3 Crew were lost.
BUFFALO (2)	4106 2583	379.5 49.2 27.4	Earle's Hull 1907	Sunk 18.6.1917, torpedoed by submarine U-70, 80 miles N.W. of Cape Wrath, 59.34 N 07.30.W. On passage Hull — New York.
HULL	1132 451	255.7 36.2 14.8	Caledon SB Co. Dundee 1907	Built for Wilson's & North Eastern Railway Shipping Co. Interned at Kiel 1914 — 1918. Returned to Ellerman's Wilson Line 28.2.1919. Sold 11.6.1937, to Societe Algerienne De Nav Pour Afrique du Nord. Algiers. Renamed *VILLE DE DJIDJELLI*. Scrapped 1955.
KOVNO (2)	1985 1102	318.0 41.1 18.3	Earle's Hull 1907	Sold 11.4.1929, to Polish-British Shipping Co. Gdynia. Renamed *LODZ*. Scrapped 1934 in Germany.
TOSNO	2000 1110	318.0 41.1 18.3	Earle's Hull 1907	Sold 14.6.1915, to the Russian Government. Absorbed into U.S.S.R. Government Fleet. Unlisted from 1927, possibly scrapped due to being damaged.
YORK	1132 451	255.7 36.2 14.8	Caledon SB Co. Dundee 1907	Built for Wilson's & North Eastern Railway Shipping Co. Sold 11.6.1937, to Societe Algerienne de Nav. Pour Afrique du Nord, Algiers. Renamed *VILLE DE BOUGIE*. Scrapped 1955.
GALILEO (2)	4768 3064	410.0 49.0 27.6	Northumber-land SB Co. Newcastle, 1908	Badly damaged 28.8.1926, by explosion and fire at New York and subsequently scrapped.
HIDALGO (2)	4271 2761	380.0 49.0 18.0	Northumber-land SB Co. Newcastle 1908	Sunk 28.8.1917, torpedoed by submarine U-28, 20 miles N.E of the North Cape, Norway. On passage Archangel — London. 15 crew were lost.
RINALDO (2)	4321 2792	385.0 49.8 18.4	Russell & Co. Pt. Glasgow 1908	Sunk 18.4.1917, torpedoed by submarine U-32. 18 miles N.W. of Cape Shershel. On passage Tees — Bombay.

ss. *CAVALLO (2)* 1922-1941

ENGINE:	3 cyl. Triple expansion
MADE BY:	Earle's Shipbuilding & Eng. Co. Ltd. Hull.
POWER:	373 NHP
2 BOILERS	200lb per sq.in.
SPEED:	10½ knots
SERVICE:	Mediterranean.
PASSENGERS:	Nil.

ss. *SPERO (2)* 1922-1959

ENGINE:	3 cyl. Triple expansion
MADE BY:	Earle's Ship-building & Eng. Co. Ltd. Hull.
POWER:	208 NHP
2 BOILERS	225lb per sq.in.
SPEED:	13 knots
SERVICE:	Copenhagen.
PASSENGERS:	42 — 1st Class. 18 — 2nd.

ss. *ERATO (3)* 1923-1941

ENGINE:	3 cyl. Triple expansion
MADE BY:	W. Beardmore & Co. Ltd. Coatbridge.
POWER:	207 NHP
2 BOILERS	225lb per sq.in.
SPEED:	11 knots
SERVICE:	Scandinavia.
PASSENGERS:	12 — 1st Class.

ss. *KYNO (2)* 1924-1940

ENGINE:	3 cyl. Triple expansion
MADE BY:	Earle's Shipbuilding & Eng. Co. Ltd. Hull.
POWER:	381 NHP
2 BOILERS	225lb per sq.in.
SPEED:	10½ knots
SERVICE:	North America.
PASSENGERS:	Nil.

NAME FORMER NAMES	GROSS NET	LENGTH BREADTH DEPTH	BUILDER PLACE YEAR	OTHER DETAILS
AARO (1)	2603 1618	301.2 41.3 25.3	Earle's Hull 1909	Sunk 1.8.1916, torpedoed by submarine U-20. On passage Hull — Cristiania. 3 crew were lost, the survivors were taken prisoner.
BASSANO (2)	4296 2763	385.1 49.8 26.4	Russell & Co. Pt. Glasgow 1909	Sold 9.12.1932, to Sturlese & Co. Spezia. Scrapped 1933 in Italy.
KELSO (2)	1292 750	250.0 35.2 15.9	Earle's Hull 1909	Sunk 19.6.1917, torpedoed by submarine UC-75 33 miles W.S.W. of Bishop Rock. On passage Oporto — London.
LIVORNO (2)	1911 1079	300.2 42.5 17.6	Earle's Hull 1909	Sold 3.4.1935, to Hellenic Lines Greece. Renamed *TURKIA*. Lost by fire 17.5.1941 near Suez.
NERO (2)	1257 709	250.0 35.2 15.7	Earle's Hull 1909	Abandoned 31.1.1920, in Bay of Biscay, on passage Swansea — Lisbon. Drifted ashore on Pierris Noires, near Brest. Declared a constructive total loss.
THURSO (2)	1244 729	250.8 34.3 15.8	Dobson & Co. Newcastle 1909	27.9.1916, captured by submarine U-44, 60 miles N.E. of Raattry Head, and sunk by gunfire. On passage Archangel — Hull. The Master and Chief Engineer were taken as prisoners.
ARIOSTO (2)	4315 2760	380.0 49.0 26.4	Northumber- land SB Co. Newcastle, 1910	Sold 5.7.1932, to Paolo Preves, London, for scrapping at Trieste. Renamed *ARIA*.
COMO (2)	1246 704	250.2 35.2 15.7	Earle's Hull 1910	Transferred 1926, to Ellerman Lines. Returned to Ellerman's Wilson Line 1930. Sold 1945, to J. Carlbom, Hull, renamed *NEKLON*. Sold 1954, renamed *KERENPE* (Turkish). Scrapped in 1959.
DARLINGTON	1076 425	255.0 36.0 17.4	Earle's Hull 1910	Built for Wilson's & North Eastern Railway Shipping Co. Renamed *CASTRO (4)* 1935. Sold 25.10.1937, to Stanhope S.S. Co. London. Renamed *STANROCK*. Sold 1937, renamed *LYDIA* (Panama). Sold 1938, renamed *OCU* (″). Sold 1938, renamed *ILOWA* (″). Sold 1939, renamed *SONA* (″). Sunk 1941, by Luftwaffe, at Adamas Bay, Milos, Greece.

NAME FORMER NAMES	GROSS NET	LENGTH BREADTH DEPTH	BUILDER PLACE YEAR	OTHER DETAILS
ESKIMO	3326 1636	331.2 45.2 25.6	Earle's Hull 1910	9.12.1914 taken over by the Royal Navy, renamed H.M.S. *ESKIMO* (M.75) 10th Cruiser Sqdn. Guns: four 6″ and two 6 pdrs. Returned to Wilson Line 18.7.1915. Captured 26.7.1916, by the German Auxiliary Cruiser *MOWE*, Risor, Norway. Returned to Ellerman's Wilson Line 19.1.1919. Sold 1921, to French owners. Scrapped in 1929.
FRANCISCO (2)	4760 3051	410.0 52.0 27.8	Northumberland SB Co. Newcastle, 1910	Sold 26.3.1935, to Leeds Shipping Co. Ltd., Cardiff. For scrapping in Italy.
MARENGO (2)	4832 3115	410.0 52.0 27.8	Northumberland SB Co. Newcastle, 1910	Sold 25.2.1935, to Paolo Preves, London. For scrapping in Italy.
BAYARDO	3471 1897	331.0 47.0 24.6	Earle's Hull 1911	Wrecked 21.1.1912, in the River Humber. Whilst on passage Gothenburg — Hull.
BORODINO (2)	2004 1091	318.0 42.2 17.2	Earle's Hull 1911	Laid down as *TSARSKOE SELO*. Chartered 1914, by the Royal Navy for use as a depot ship at Scapa flow. Returned to Ellerman's Wilson Line in 1919. Sold 26.9.1939, to the Admiralty. Sunk 27.5.1940, as a block ship at Zeebrugge.
CASTRO (2)	1228 700	250.2 35.2 15.9	Earle's Hull 1911	Detained at Hamburg, August 1914. taken over by the German Navy and Renamed *LIBUA*. Scuttled 22.4.1916, off Daunt's Rock, to avoid capture, whilst disguised as a Norwegian vessel.
ERATO (2)	2041 1133	301.1 43.1 20.5	Clyde SB Co. Pt. Glasgow 1911	Sunk 1.9.1917, struck a mine laid by submarine UC-69. 4 miles S.E. of Lizard, Cornwall. On passage Dunkirk — Barry Roads.
GOURKO	1975 1073	318.0 42.2 17.3	Earle's Hull 1911	Chartered to Royal Navy August 1914. Used as an amenity/theatre ship at Scapa Flow. Returned to Ellerman's Wilson Line in 1919. Sold 21.5.1940 to the Admiralty. Sunk 4.6.1940, as a block ship at Dunkirk.
HARROGATE (1)	1168 477	255.1 36.1 15.1	Earle's Hull 1911	Built for Wilson's & North Eastern Railway Shipping Co. Foundered 20.2.1918, 30 miles off Norway. On passage Hull — Bergen.
HYDRO (2)	1228 700	250.2 36.1 15.9	Earle's Hull 1911	Capsized 22.1.1915, off Rathlin Island. On passage Liverpool — Trondheim. Heavy seas washed away hatch covers. Abandoned 9 p.m. 21st, 14 crew lost.

ss. _SALERNO (4)_ 1924-1956

ENGINE:	3 cyl. Triple expansion
MADE BY:	Earle's Ship-building & Eng. Co. Ltd. Hull.
POWER:	160 NHP
2 BOILERS	225lb per sq.in.
SPEED:	11 knots
SERVICE:	Scandinavia.
PASSENGERS:	4 — 1st Class.

ss. _TEANO (2)_ 1925-1943

ENGINE:	3 cyl. Triple expansion
MADE BY:	Earle's Ship-building & Eng. Co. Ltd. Hull.
POWER:	137 NHP
2 BOILERS	225lb per sq.in.
SPEED:	10 knots
SERVICE:	Continent.
PASSENGERS:	4 — 1st Class.

ss. *CONSUELLO (2)* 1937-1963

ENGINE:	3 cyl. Triple expansion
MADE BY:	Swan, Hunter & Wigham Richardson, Newcastle.
POWER:	786 NHP
4 BOILERS	225lb per sq.in.
SPEED:	13 knots
SERVICE:	North America.
PASSENGERS:	6 — 1st Class.

ss. *PALERMO (2)* 1938-1965

ENGINE:	3 cyl. Triple expansion
MADE BY:	Cent. Marine Eng. Works, Hartlepool.
POWER:	465 NHP
2 BOILERS	225lb per sq.in.
SPEED:	12 knots
SERVICE:	North America, Mediterranean.
PASSENGERS:	4 — 1st Class.

NAME FORMER NAMES	GROSS NET	LENGTH BREADTH DEPTH	BUILDER PLACE YEAR	OTHER DETAILS
MONTEBELLO (2)	4324 2770	385.0 50.5 27.2	Earle's Hull 1911	Sunk 21.6.1918, torpedoed by submarine U-100, 320 miles west of Ushant. On passage London — Baltimore. 41 crew including the Master were lost.
TINTO (1)	795 412	200.1 32.1 13.4	Dundee SB Dundee 1911	Sold 13.1.1937, to Dampskslsk Hetland A/S, Copenhagen. Renamed *KONGEAA*. Sold 1939, renamed *HERMES* (Finnish). Sold 1951, renamed *BRANDO* (Finnish). Scrapped 1955 at Altona.
ALBANO (2)	1176 519	250.2 37.2 14.7	Earle's Hull 1912	Sunk 2.3.1940, mined off Coquet Island. 4 miles east of Hartlepool. 9 crew including the Master were lost. 10 survivors picked up by destroyer escort and 8 more by the Hull trawler *STELLA CARINA*.
CATTARO (1)	1901 1130	300.0 44.6 17.8	Earle's Hull 1912	Sunk 26.6.1917, torpedoed by submarine U-62, 130 miles W.S.W. of Bishop Rock. 48.50 N 07.47 W. On passage Civita Vecchia — Hull.
GRODNO (2)	1955 988	295.2 43.2 17.2	Clyde SB Co. Pt. Glasgow 1912	12.8.1915, captured by submarine U-22, 98 miles N.W of the Lofoten Islands and sunk by torpedo. On passage Archangel — Hull.
SALERNO (3)	2071 1149	300.6 44.7 17.9	Dunlop Bremner Pt. Glasgow 1912	Sunk 14.10.1915, struck a mine laid by submarine UC-3. 2 miles south of Long Sand Lightvessel. On passage Aalborg — Tyne — Santos.
SERBINO	2205 1211	310.3 44.7 17.9	Dunlop Bremner Pt. Glasgow 1912	Sunk 16.8.1915, torpedoed by submarine U-9, off Worms lighthouse (Baltic). On passage Riga — Petrograd.
SORRENTO (2)	1899 1124	300.0 44.7 17.8	Earle's Hull 1912	Sold 21.11.1938, to Maritime Lloyd, Haifa, Palestine. Renamed *MIRIAM*. Wrecked 2.2.1944, near Cape Otranto.
TORCELLO (1)	1900 1129	300.0 44.7 17.8	Earle's Hull 1912	Sunk 15.7.1917, torpedoed by submarine U-48, 160 miles S.W. of Bishop Rock. On passage Palermo — Hull. 1 crewman lost.
VARRO (TUG)	196 —	100.3 25.6 11.3	Goole SB Co. Goole 1912	Sold 16.11.1946, to Loucas Matsos & Son, Piraeus. Renamed *LOUCAS MATSOS*. Scrapped 1984, at Perama.
CARLO (1)	1987 1181	310.0 44.6 17.9	Clyde SB & Eng. Pt. Glasgow, 1913	Sunk 13.11.1917 torpedoed by submarine U-95, 7 miles S by W of the Coninbeg Lightvessel. On passage Carthegena — Liverpool. 2 crewman lost.

NAME FORMER NAMES	GROSS NET	LENGTH BREADTH DEPTH	BUILDER PLACE YEAR	OTHER DETAILS
CAVALLO (1)	2086 1107	310.3 44.7 17.9	Dunlop Bremner Pt. Glasgow 1913	Sunk 1.2.1918, torpedoed by submarine U-46, 6 miles N.W. of Trevose Head. On passage Liverpool — Swansea — Odda. 3 crew were lost.
GITANO (2)	1179 519	250.4 37.2 14.7	Earle's Hull 1913	Posted missing Jan. 1919, lost with all hands, presumed mined after passing Flamborough Head 20.12.1918. On passage Hull — Gothenburg.
GUIDO (1)	2093 1106	310.0 44.8 18.0	Dunlop Bremner Pt. Glasgow 1913	8.6.1915, Captured by submarine U-25, 27 miles N.E. of Rattray Head and sunk by torpedo. On passage Hull — Archangel.
KYNO (1)	2202 1232	310.3 44.7 17.9	Dunlop Bremner Pt. Glasgow 1913	Sunk 16.11.1917, torpedoed by submarine U-63, 9 miles N.E. off Cape Shershel, Algeria. On passage Hull — Alexandria. 5 crew were lost.
POLO (2)	1906 1127	300.0 44.7 17.8	Earle's Hull 1913	Sunk 12.2.1918, torpedoed by submarine UB-57, 6 miles S.E. by S. off St. Catherines. On passage Hull — Alexandria. 3 crew were lost.
SILVIO (2)	1284 651	260.7 36.2 15.4	Dundee SB Co. Dundee 1913	Badly damaged 21.12.1940, by air attack at Liverpool, subsequently scrapped. 2 crewmen were killed during the raid. Cargo discharged by diver. Wreck cleared 1947.
TEANO (1)	1906 1126	300.0 44.7 17.8	Earle's Hull 1913	29.6.1916. Captured by submarine U-35 and scuttled 24 miles N.W. by N. from Marittimo Island, Sicily. On passage Hull — Naples.
CANNIZARO	6133 3899	420.0 53.4 33.4	Northumber- land SB Co. Newcastle, 1914	Sunk 28.3.1917, torpedoed by submarine U-24 145 miles S.S.W. of Fastnet. 49.00 N 10.00 W. On passage New York — Hull.
COLORADO (2)	5652 3566	423.6 55.8 31.4	Russell & Co. Pt. Glasgow 1914	Sunk 20.10.1917, torpedoed by submarine UB-31, 1.5 miles off Start Point. On passage Hull — Alexandria. 4 crew were lost.
DESTRO (1)	859 393	210.2 33.1 13.9	Earle's Hull 1914	Sunk 25.3.1918, torpedoed by submarine U-96, 5 miles S.W. of the Mull of Galloway. On passage Namsos — Manchester.

ss. *ANGELO (3)* 1940-1963

ENGINE:	3 cyl. Triple expansion
MADE BY:	Swan, Hunter & Wigham Richardson, Newcastle.
POWER:	418 NHP
2 BOILERS	225lb per sq.in.
SPEED:	13 knots
SERVICE:	Copenhagen.
PASSENGERS:	12 — 1st Class.

mv. *SACREMENTO* 1945-1964

ENGINE:	2 oil 2 SA each 3 cyl.
MADE BY:	W. Doxford & Sons Ltd. Sunderland.
POWER:	5200 BHP
SPEED:	14 knots
SERVICE:	North America.
PASSENGERS:	12 — 1st Class.

ss. *ARIOSTO (4)* 1946-1967

ENGINE:	3 cyl. Triple expansion
MADE BY:	Cent. Marine Eng. Works. Hartlepool.
POWER:	2700 IHP
2 BOILERS	225lb per sq.in.
SPEED:	13½ knots
SERVICE:	Mediterranean.
PASSENGERS:	12 — 1st Class.

mv. *ELECTRO (2)* 1946-1967

ENGINE:	oil 2 SA
MADE BY:	British Polar Engines Ltd. Glasgow.
POWER:	800 BHP
SPEED:	9 knots
SERVICE:	London, Continent.
PASSENGERS:	Nil.

NAME FORMER NAMES	GROSS NET	LENGTH BREADTH DEPTH	BUILDER PLACE YEAR	OTHER DETAILS
LEPANTO (2) **CITY OF* *RIPON*	6394 4020	424.9 53.5 33.8	Russell & Co. Pt. Glasgow 1915	15.3.1917, shelled by U-Boat but escaped. Torpedoed 20.10.1917. Towed to Dartmouth and repaired. In 1934, renamed *CITY OF RIPON*. Sunk 11.11.1942, (08.01 CET) torpedoed by U-160 90 miles S.E. of Georgetown, Trinidad. 08.40 N 59.20 W. On passage Table Bay — Trinidad. With the loss of 56 crew. 27 survivors were picked up by the Brazilian vessel ss. *MIDOSI*.
URBINO (3)	6651 4240	446.0 57.3 30.9	Earle's Hull 1915	24.9.1915, captured by submarine U-41, 67 miles S.W. of Bishop Rock, and sunk by gunfire. On passage New York — Hull.
OSWEGO	5793 3702	423.5 56.0 28.7	Russell & Co. Pt. Glasgow 1916	Sunk 29.5.1917, torpedoed by submarine U-86, 175 miles west of Bishop Rock. 48.44 N 10.15 W. On passage New York — Hull.
SMOLENSK	2487 1534	286.6 40.6 26.0	Doxford & Co. Sunderland 1916	Sold 4.4.1929, to Polish-British Shipping Co. Gdynia. Renamed *WARSZAWA*. Torpedoed 26.12.1941, off Tobruk. On passage Alexandria — Tobruk, with 45 crew, 5 gunners & 416 passengers. 23 persons were lost.
CHICAGO (3)	7708 5711	446.0 57.3 30.9	Earle's Hull 1917	Sunk 8.7.1918, torpedoed by submarine UB-107, 4 miles N.E. of Flamborough Head. On passage N. Shields — Gibraltar. 3 crew were lost.
DARINO	1349 830	236.3 36.5 17.1	Ramage & Ferguson, Leith 1917	Transferred 1921, to Ellerman Lines Liverpool. Torpedoed 19.11.1939, by U-41, NW of Cape Ortegal. On passage Oporto — Liverpool. 16 crew were lost.
DOMINO (2)	1193 536	255.5 36.2 14.9	Dundee SB Co. Dundee 1917	Wrecked 4.11.1923, off Groningen lightvessel, on passage London — Oslo.
GRODNO (3)	2458 1470	303.0 43.0 20.8	Gray & Co. West Hartlepool 1919	Sold 10.7.1946 to A/S Olymp, Oslo, Renamed *MA GOO*. Sold 1947, renamed *HEDJA* (Swedish). Scrapped 1968.
POLO (3)	1950 970	290.0 42.5 18.8	Swan Hunter & Wigham Richardson, Sunderland 1919	12.1.1943, arrived at Bougie, West Africa to load lubricating oil in drums and petrol in tins. Whilst waiting to sail on 17.1.1943 an explosion occurred in the vicinity of No's 4-5 holds. The subsequent fire spread rapidly forcing the crew to abandon ship. Shore fire appliances were unable to bring the fire under control, and on the 18th, it became necessary to tow the vessel out of port. By the 19th, the *POLO* was totally burnt out and was sunk by gunfire in deep water. All the crew were saved.

NAME FORMER NAMES	GROSS NET	LENGTH BREADTH DEPTH	BUILDER PLACE YEAR	OTHER DETAILS
THURSO (3) x *WAR BRAMBLE*	2436 1451	313.5 43.0 20.8	Austin & Sons Sunderland 1919	Sunk 15.6.1942, (04.33 CET) torpedoed by U-552, N.E. of the Azores, 43.41 N 18.02 W. In convoy HG.84 on passage Lisbon — Liverpool. 13 crew were lost. 29 survivors picked up by one of the escorting corvettes.
TRENTINO (1)	3079 1845	310.0 44.7 26.8	Dundee SB Co. Dundee 1919	Sunk 8.5.1941, during air raid at Langton Dock, Liverpool. Set on fire by direct hit H.E. Bomb and incendiaries. Refloated 30.5.1941, towed to Pluckington Bank, Kings Dock River wall for scrapping.
URBINO (4)	5199 3212	400.4 52.2 28.5	Earle's Hull 1919	Laid down as wartime standard vessel *WAR SEAL*. From 1934 managed by Ellerman Bucknall Line. Sold 2.4.1954, to Br. Iron & Steel Co. for scrapping at Faslane.
DESTRO (2)	3553 2177	314.0 45.2 28.7	Dunlop Bremner Pt. Glasgow 1920	Transferred 1925, to Ellerman Lines, Liverpool. Damaged by bombs 27.3.1942 at Tobruk. 1946, renamed *DESTRIAN*. Sold 1950, renamed *PERGOMON* (German). Sold 1963, for scrapping at Bremerhaven.
DIDO (3)	3554 2175	314.0 45.2 28.7	Dunlop Bremner Pt. Glasgow 1920	Transferred 1925, to Ellerman Lines. Taken at Brest 18.6.1940, renamed *DORPAT*. Mined 11.4.1943, at Aarhus, salved. Sunk 3.5.1945, by air attack. Salvaged and sold to Finnish owners. Renamed *LEILA*. Sold 11.1963, for scrapping in Finland.
DYNAMO (2)	809 377	186.3 29.4 12.4	Williamson Workington 1920	Mined 17.4.1943, at Barrow Deep, Thames Estuary near B8 buoy. 4 crew & 3 gunners were lost. 13 survivors were picked up by escort destroyer. Wreck dispersed by December 1943.
GUIDO (2)	3921 2396	333.0 46.6 29.0	Goole SB & E Goole 1920	Sunk 8.3.1943, (08.55 GMT) torpedoed by unknown U-Boat, 45 miles S.E. of Cape Farewell. 58.08 N. 32.20 W in convoy SC.121. On passage St. Kitts — Greenock. 10 crew were lost, 35 survivors were picked up by U.S.S. *SPENCER*.
RUNO (2)	1858 1089	262.7 39.0 16.6	Ramage & Ferguson Leith, 1920	Sunk 11.4.1943, (00.22 CET) torpedoed by U-593 west of Maderia, 32.15 N 23.55 E. On passage Benghazi — Alexandria. 16 crew were lost. 21 survivors were picked up by the corvette H.M.S.*DELPHINIUM*
CALYPSO (3) x *ALEXANDRA WOERMANN* x *BRUXELLES-VILLE*	3820 2382	358.1 44.2 23.4	Raylton Dixon Middlesbrough 1898	Bought 4.11.1920, from the Shipping Controller. x German, Woermann Line. Renamed *CALYPSO (3)* Sold 13.11.1936, for scrapping at Ghent.

ss. *DOMINO (4)* 1947-1962

ENGINE:	3 cyl. Triple expansion
MADE BY:	Ailsa Ship-building Co. Ltd. Troon.
POWER:	2350 IHP
2 BOILERS	225lb per sq.in.
SPEED:	13½ knots
SERVICE:	Mediterranean.
PASSENGERS:	12 — 1st Class.

Photograph courtesy of Fotoflite.

ss. *LEO (3)* 1947-1967

ENGINE:	3 cyl. Triple expansion
MADE BY:	Swan, Hunter & Wigham Richardson, Newcastle.
POWER:	1900 IHP
2 BOILERS	210lb per sq.in.
SPEED:	13½ knots
SERVICE:	Scandinavia, Mediterranean.
PASSENGERS:	12 — 1st Class.

Photograph courtesy of Fotoflite.

ss. *RIALTO (2)* 1949-1970

ENGINE:	3 cyl. Triple expansion
MADE BY:	Swan, Hunter & Wigham Richardson, Newcastle.
POWER:	4200 IHP
4 BOILERS	225lb per sq.in.
SPEED:	13½ knots
SERVICE:	North America.
PASSENGERS:	6 — 1st Class.

ss. *BORODINO (3)* 1950-1967

ENGINE:	3 cyl. Triple expansion & L P turbine
MADE BY:	Ailsa Ship-building Co. Ltd. Troon.
POWER:	2450 IHP
2 BOILERS	225lb per sq.in.
SPEED:	13½ knots
SERVICE:	Copenhagen.
PASSENGERS:	36 — 1st Class.

NAME FORMER NAMES	GROSS NET	LENGTH BREADTH DEPTH	BUILDER PLACE YEAR	OTHER DETAILS
CARLO (2) x LAS PALMAS	1737 985	277.7 39.2 17.9	Henry Koch Lubeck 1911	Bought 15.10.1920, from the Shipping Controller. x German, Oldenburg — Portuguese Line. Renamed CARLO (3). Sold 1939, to the Royal Navy for use as an ammunition hulk. Scrapped 1951, at Port Glasgow.
CATO (2) x FINK	1460 855	230.9 36.8 15.0	Stettiner Oderwerke 1913	Bought 4.11.1920, from the Shipping Controller. x German, Rud. Christ Gribel Line. Renamed CATO (2). Sold 2.5.1938, to Salvagno Anonima Nav. Venice. Renamed ANDREA CONTARINI. Sold 1957, renamed SILA (Italian). Scrapped 1965.
KATIE	2423 1316	296.0 43.2 19.2	Elsinor SB Helsingors 1900	Bought 20.4.1920, from the Shipping Controller x Russian, Russisch — Baltische D.G. Sold 13.8.1922, back to the Russian Baltic S.S. Co., Riga. Sold 1935, renamed VICTORIA (Finnish). Sold 1937, renamed INARI, 1942, renamed LAILA 1948, renamed LAILA NURMINEN, (Finnish) 1949, renamed ELSA S (Finnish). Scrapped 1959.
LEO (2) x SPES	1127 641	225.7 35.4 14.4	Stettiner Oderwerke Stettin 1908	Bought 29.12.1920, from the Shipping Controller. x German, Rud. Christ Gribel. Line. Renamed LEO (2). Sunk 25.7.1940, during air attack off Dover. On passage Seaham — Portsmouth. 6 crew were lost, 21 were rescued.
MANCHURIAN x TILLY RUSS	2768 1751	292.1 41.3 25.7	A.G. Neptun Rostock 1905	Bought 24.11.1920, from the Shipping Controller. x German, Ernst Russ, Line.Renamed MANCHURIAN. Transferred 1925, to Ellerman Lines. Sold 14.3.1935, to Ward's for scrapping at Milford Haven.
ORLANDO (2) x INANDA	4233 2584	370.0 46.2 18.5	Hall Russell Aberdeen 1904	Bought 4.6.1920, from Charante S.S. Co. Liverpool. Renamed ORLANDO. Sold 7.7.1932 to T.W. Ward for scrapping at Briton Ferry.
ROLLO (2) x ITALIAN x FANTEE	3658 2802	345.0 44.0 14.2	Barclay Curle Glasgow 1899	Transferred from Ellerman City Line 1920. Renamed ROLLO. Laid up at Hull in July 1928. Sold 28.9.1932, to Petersen & Albeck, for scrapping at Copenhagen.
TORCELLO (2) x STAHLOF	1479 875	231.7 36.4 14.7	Stettiner Oderwerke Stettin, 1911	Bought 18.10.1920, from the Shipping Controller. x German, Nene Dampfer Co. A.G. Renamed TORCELLO (2). Sold 15.10.1938, to Italian owners. Renamed LUTINE. Torpedoed 17.1.1943, by H.M.S. UNSEEN.

NAME FORMER NAMES	GROSS NET	LENGTH BREADTH DEPTH	BUILDER PLACE YEAR	OTHER DETAILS
VASCO (2) x *BRANDEN-BURG*	2166 1233	283.6 41.2 18.8	Stettiner Oderwerke Stettin 1910	Bought 15.11.1920, from the Shipping Controller. x. German, H.G. Stevenson, Akt. Ges. Renamed *VASCO (2)*. Sold 18.11.1929, to F. L. Nimtz, Stettin, renamed *FRANZ JURGEN*. Sunk 10.4.1945, during air raid on Kiel by R.A.F. Salved 1949. 1954 renamed *HANS BERNSTEIN* (German). Sold 1969 for scrapping.
IAGO (2) x *SANTA FE*	5342 2818	388.5 47.8 18.8	C.S. Swan Hunter Newcastle 1901	Bought 25.5.1921, from the Shipping Controller. x German. Hamburg Sud-America Line. Renamed *IAGO (2)*. Sold 23.1.1922, back to Hamburg Sud-America Line and renamed *SANTA FE*. Sold 1932, for scrapping.
CHEMNITZ	7681 4784	482.2 54.3 39.7	Tecklenborg Geestemunde 1901	Bought 9.1.1921, from the Shipping Controller. x German, Norddeutscher Lloyd Line. Sold 27.11.1933 to N.V. Simons'Ijzer, Rotterdam for scrapping in Holland.
GITANO (3)	3956 2460	333.0 46.6 20.4	Goole SB & E Goole 1921	Sold 23.8.1955, to B.I. & Steel Co. For scrapping at Rosyth.
CAVALLO (2)	2268 1304	312.0 44.7 18.7	Dundee SB Co. Dundee 1922	Sunk 25.4.1941, during air attack at Nauplia, Greece. Bombed 23, 24 & 25th. All 40 crew & 7 gunners saved.
CITO (2)	692 369	179.0 28.1 12.9	Swan Hunter Wigham Richardson Sunderland, 1922	Sold 16.3.1937, to United Africa Co. London. Renamed *AKASSIAN*. Wrecked 31.10.1938, near Addah.
DRACO (2)	2017 1177	274.7 39.3 18.5	Hall Russell Aberdeen 1922	Beached 11.4.1941, damaged during air attack at Tobruk. 1 gunner lost. Bombed again 21st and became total loss. Salved in 1948. Scrapped at Valencia. (13.9.1948).
SELBY	1039 541	228.1 34.2 13.8	Duthie Torry Aberdeen 1922	Built for Wilson's & North Eastern Railway Shipping Co. Sold 21.5.1958, for scrapping at Odense.
SPERO (2)	1589 817	257.0 37.0 17.0	Dundee SB Co. Dundee 1922	14.9.1947. Damaged by a mine explosion, off Danish Coast. Put into Aalborg for repairs then to Dry dock at Hull for overhaul. Sold 24.9.1959, for scrapping in Belgium.

mv. *CAVALLO (3)* 1951-1971

ENGINE:	2 oil 2 SA each 8 cyl.
MADE BY:	British Polar Engines Ltd. Glasgow.
POWER:	3040 BHP
SPEED:	13½ knots
SERVICE:	Mediterranean.
PASSENGERS:	12 — 1st Class.

ss. *CICERO (2)* 1954-1970

ENGINE:	3 cyl. Triple expansion
MADE BY:	Swan, Hunter & Wigham Richardson, Newcastle.
POWER:	2460 IHP
2 BOILERS	225lb per sq.in.
SPEED:	13½ knots
SERVICE:	Gothenburg.
PASSENGERS:	12 — 1st Class.

ss. *TEANO (3)* 1955-1968

ENGINE:	3 cyl. Triple expansion
MADE BY:	Swan, Hunter & Wigham Richardson, Newcastle.
POWER:	1900 IHP
2 BOILERS	210lb per sq.in.
SPEED:	13½ knots
SERVICE:	Scandinavia.
PASSENGERS:	12 — 1st Class.

mv. *AARO (2)* 1960-1972

ENGINE:	oil 2 SA 7 cyl. Sulzer.
MADE BY:	Fairfield Shipbuilding & Eng. Co. Ltd. Glasgow.
POWER:	3500 BHP
SPEED:	13½ knots
SERVICE:	Copenhagen.
PASSENGERS:	12 — 1st Class.

NAME FORMER NAMES	GROSS NET	LENGTH BREADTH DEPTH	BUILDER PLACE YEAR	OTHER DETAILS
TASSO (3)	3569 2138	344.4 42.8 28.2	Ramage & Ferguson Leith, 1922	Sold 15.4.1929, to Polish-British S.S. Co. Gdynia. Renamed *PREMJER*. Sold 1935, to Lloyd Trestino, Italy. Renamed *ADUA*. Sunk 4.4.1941 war loss.
TRURO (2)	974 548	228.0 34.2 13.8	Duthie Torry Aberdeen 1922	Sunk 15.9.1939 (18.30 GMT), north of Fraserburgh by U-36 with gun & torpedo. On passage Hull — Stavanger. Crew rescued by Belgian trawler *VANVLAADEREN* and landed at Aberdeen.
COLORADO (3)	6614 4223	433.0 57.4 30.2	W. Gray & Co. Sunderland 1923	Transferred 1925, to Hall Line. Renamed *CITY OF OSAKA*. Wrecked 22.9.1930, Buchaness, near Aberdeen.
ERATO (3)	1335 735	247.3 36.2 14.6	Duthie Torry Aberdeen 1923	Sunk 28.7.1941, (23.51 CET), torpedoed by U-126, west of Cape Finisterre. 43.10 N 17.30 W. In convoy OG.69. On passage Liverpool — Oporto. 9 crew were lost. 27 survivors picked up by H.M.S. *BEGONIA* convoy escort.
CITY OF *HONG KONG*	9606 6071	470.2 61.5 32.2	Earle's Hull 1924	Laid down as *COLORADO (4)*. Transferred 20.5.1925 to Ellerman Lines. During the 1939-1945 war served as a troopship. Sold 1951, to a F. G. Armator, Genoa. Renamed *CENTUARO*. Sold 1955, for scrapping at Savora.
KELSO (3)	3956 2426	332.8 46.6 14.2	Goole SB & E Goole 1924	Sunk 8.8.1942, (13.25 GMT), torpedoed by U-176, S.E. of Cape Farewell, 56.30 N 32.14 W. In convoy SC.94. On passage New York — Sydney N.S. — Liverpool. 3 crew were lost. 42 survivors were picked up by the corvette H.M.S. *BATTLEFORT*.
KYNO (2)	3950 2442	332.8 46.6 20.4	Goole SB & E Goole 1924	Sunk 28.8.1940, (20.57 CET), torpedoed by U-28, N.W. of St. Kilda 58.06 N 13.26 W. On passage New York — Hull. 5 crew were lost. 32 survivors rescued.
NERO (3) x *CLADDAGH* x *TRUTHFUL* x *SUSSEX* *COAST*	640 280	180.0 28.5 12.6	Harkess & Sons Middlesbrough 1907	Bought 25.11.1924 from City of Cork Steam Packet Company. Renamed *NERO*. Sold 31.11.1927 to General Steam Navigation Co. Sold 1928, renamed *IMOLA* (Italian). Sunk 13.3.1936, following explosion in the Red Sea, as *MARCHIGIANO* (Italian).
SALERNO (4)	869 362	215.7 32.8 14.10	Earle's Hull 1924	Captured 15.4.1940, by Germans at Sandafjord. Renamed *MARKIRCH*. Retaken at Eckernfjord 1945. Renamed *EMPIRE* *SALERNO*. Returned to Ellerman's Wilson Line 6.7.1946. Renamed *SALERNO*. Sold 14.11.1956, renamed *TAXIARCHIS* (Greek). Sold 1959, for scrapping at Perama.

NAME FORMER NAMES	GROSS NET	LENGTH BREADTH DEPTH	BUILDER PLACE YEAR	OTHER DETAILS
SALMO (2)	1269 621	237.7 35.3 15.8	Swan Hunter & Wigham Richardson Newcastle, 1924	Captured 3.7.1940, by Vichy French at Casa Blanca. Renamed ST.EMILE. Scuttled 16.12.1942, as a blockship at Port Lyaute. Scrapping of wreck commenced in 1943.
DOMINO (3)	1453 711	255.3 36.1 16.7	New Waterway SB. Schiedam 1925	Damaged by fire 3/4.5.1941, during air raid at Canada Dock, Liverpool. Capsized 5.4.1941. Salved and left dock on 22.9.1941 to be scrapped at New Ferry.
HARROGATE (2)	1029 552	240.4 33.9 14.2	Ramage & Ferguson Leith, 1925	Built for Wilson's & North Eastern Railway Shipping Co. Sold 2.6.1958, for scrapping at Rotterdam.
TEANO (2)	762 299	195.1 31.1 13.2	Earle's Hull 1925	Lost 8.11.1943, in collision with ss. CHYBASSA in the River Humber, whilst on passage Hull — London. One crewman was lost.
BASSANO (3)	4834 2687	419.6 55.8 25.7	Swan Hunter & Wigham Richardson Newcastle, 1937	Sunk 9.1.1941 (18.14 CET), torpedoed by U-105 N.W. of Rockall, 57.57 N 17.42 W. On passage New York — Glasgow. 1 crewman lost. 49 crew, 2 gunners and 5 passengers were rescued.
CONSUELLO (2)	4871 2583	419.6 55.8 25.7	Swan Hunter & Wigham Richardson Newcastle, 1937	Sold 4.7.1963, to Grosvenor Shipping Co. London. Renamed GROSVENOR DISCOVERER. Sold 11.1964 for scrapping at Hong Kong, after being laid up at that port.
PALERMO (2)	2838 1401	354.8 48.1 22.1	W. Gray & Co. West Hartlepool 1938	Sold 13.7.1965, to Roussos Bros. Piraeus. Renamed KYMA. Sold 1972, for scrapping in Turkey. Arrived Fener (Golden Horn) 6.7.1972.
TASSO (4)	1586 768	295.2 40.2 15.8	Swan Hunter & Wigham Richardson Newcastle, 1938	Sunk 2.12.1940 (18.25 CET), torpedoed by U-94, S.W. of Rockall. 55.06 N 18.04 W. In convoy HX.90 on passage Bermuda — Oban. 27 survivors rescued by H.M.S. VISCOUNT. 5 crew lost.
VOLO (2)	1587 768	295.2 40.2 15.8	Swan Hunter & Wigham Richardson Newcastle, 1938	Sunk 28.12.1941, (02.53 GMT), torpedoed by U-75, off Mersa Matruh. On passage Tobruk — Alexandria. 24 crew lost. 11 survivors rescued by a R.N. Lighter & H.M.S. LEGION.

NAME FORMER NAMES	GROSS NET	LENGTH BREADTH DEPTH	BUILDER PLACE YEAR	OTHER DETAILS
FORTO (TUG)	180 —	107.8 25.8 —	Cook Welton & Gemmell Beverley, 1939	Sold 13.3.1968, to United Towing Co. Hull. Sold 24.6.1968, for scrapping at Blyth.
VASCO (3)	2829 1416	354.8 48.1 22.1	W. Gray & Co. West Hartlepool 1939	Sold 12.8.1963, to Union Enterprise S. Co. Piraeus. Renamed *BROOKFIELD*. Sold 1969, renamed *EVANGELOS Z.* (Cyprus). Sold 1973, for scrapping in Yugoslavia. Demolition commenced 21.6.1973 at Split.
ANGELO (2)	2209 980	306.2 44.2 19.7	Swan Hunter & Wigham Richardson Newcastle, 1940	Sold 22.2.1963, to S. Lalis & P. Loizos. Pireaus. Renamed *NEVADA II* then *SPYROS L.* Laid up at Pireaus from 15.2.1971. Sold 1972, renamed *MANOS* (Greek). Sold 1973, for scrapping in Greece, arrived at Pireaus 3.1973.
ARIOSTO (3)	2176 979	306.2 44.2 19.7	Swan Hunter & Wigham Richardson Newcastle, 1940	Sunk 24.10.1941, (06.37 CET), torpedoed by U-564 S.W. of Cape St. Vincent, 36.20 N 10.50 W. In convoy HG.75. On passage Lisbon — Liverpool. 6 crew were lost. 2 survivors were picked up by H.M.S. *HELIOTROPE*, 40 by ss. *PACIFIC*.
CATTARO (2)	2901 1379	355.6 48.1 22.1	W. Gray & Co. West Hartlepool 1945	Sold 6.2.1966, to Manovas Shipping Co. Panama. Renamed *VRACHOS*. 10.1.1971, engine room badly damaged by fire whilst at Galatz, Rumania. Beached Sulina Canal. Declared constructive total loss. The vessel was not insured and was abandoned to the Rumanian Government who sold her for scrap, to meet their expenses.
SACRAMENTO m.v.	7096 4012	451.0 58.9 28.3	Cammell Laird Birkenhead 1945	Transferred 1964, to Ellerman Bucknall. Renamed *CITY OF BRISTOL*. Sold 1969, renamed *FELICIE* (Cyprus). Sold 1970, renamed 30th DE NOVIEMBRE (Cuba). Sold 1977, for scrapping at Faslane, arrived 27.7.1977.
TASSO (5)	1598 740	295.2 40.2 17.0	Swan Hunter & Wigham Richardson Newcastle, 1945	Sold 21.10.1963, to Chr. M. Sarlis & Co. Patras. Renamed *SOPHIA*. Sold 1972, for scrapping in Greece. Arrived Parama 14.8.1972.
ARIOSTO (4)	2208 965	306.8 44.2 19.7	W. Gray & Co. West Hartlepool 1946	Sold 2.8.1967 to Jos. Boel & Zonen, Tamise. For scrapping in Belgium.

NAME FORMER NAMES	GROSS NET	LENGTH BREADTH DEPTH	BUILDER PLACE YEAR	OTHER DETAILS
BASSANO (4)	4986 2647	419.7 55.9 25.6	Swan Hunter & Wigham Richardson Newcastle, 1946	Sold 17.7.1967, to Greek Sea Shipping Co. Panama. Renamed ATHANASIA. Sold 1969, for scrappng at Shanghai. Left Puco Butcum 27.9.1969.
DYNAMO (3) x KYLEBROOK x HOMEWARD	881 425	193.8 30.2 12.4	Williamson & Son Workington 1926	Bought 21.9.1944, from Northwest Shipping Co. Liverpool. Renamed DYNAMO. Sold 1956 to Holderness Shipping Co. Renamed HOLDERNOOK. Sold 1959, for scrapping in Holland, arrived at Haarlem 18.8.1959.
ELECTRO (2) m.v x WILLIAMS-TOWN	793 447	198.9 29.0 13.1	N.V. Schpsw. G. Wherf Deest 1937	Bought 1.4.1946, from Comben Longstaff & Co. Renamed ELECTRO. Sold 7.6.1967, renamed GLORGIOS (Greek). Sold 1972, renamed NICOLOS C. (Cyprus). Sank 1.2. 1972, off Pylos 36.45 N 21.25 E after being on fire, all crew saved.
LIVORNO (3)	2957 1464	355.6 50.0 22.1	W. Gray & Co. West Hartlepool 1946	Sold 25.8.1967, to Margerencia Cia Nav. SA, Panama. Renamed ANTONIS. Laid up at Genoa from 30.1.1973, Sold 1973, to Italian owners for scrapping. Renamed MAGISTER, arrived at Spezia 21.2.1973.
MALMO (2)	1779 729	297.1 42.2 17.3	W. Gray & Co. West Hartlepool 1946	Sold 10.5.1965, to Lisboa Cia Nav. Panama. Renamed AKTI. Capsized Oct. 1965, after being beached due to fire in hold, at Europort (Rotterdam), whilst on passage Massowa — Rotterdam. Subsequently salved and sold for scrap, arrived Rotterdam breakers 7.11.1966.
PRESTO (2) (TUG) x EMPIRE SARA	276 —	111.8 26.7 12.4	Cochrane & Sons Selby 1943	Bought 17.6.1946, from Ministry of War Transport. Renamed PRESTO. Sold 13.3.1968, to United Towing Co. Hull. Sold 24.6.1968, for scrapping at Blyth.
RINALDO (3)	2957 1467	355.6 50.0 22.1	W. Gray & Sons West Hartlepool 1946	Sold 21.9.1967, to United Maritime Lines Corp. Pireaus. Renamed EMERALD. Sold 1974, renamed MIDAS (Cyprus). Sold 1974, for scrapping in Yugoslavia, arrived Split 14.9.1974.
VOLO (3)	1797 712	296.10 42.2 17.2	Swan Hunter & Wigham Richardson Newcastle, 1946	Sold 20.10.1969, to Maltese National Lines, Malta, Renamed AVOLOS. Sold 1975, renamed MDINA (Italian). Sold 1979, for scrapping at Catania, Italy.
ALBANO (3)	2239 939	308.6 46.2 19.7	W. Gray & Co. West Hartlepool 1947	Sold 7.4.1962, to J.S. Webster & Sons, Cayman Islands. Renamed MAGISTER. Sold 1973, renamed PETEN (Guatemala). Out of class, 1.3.1974. Sold 1974, for scrapping in Pakistan, arrived Karachi 6.11.1974

NAME FORMER NAMES	GROSS NET	LENGTH BREADTH DEPTH	BUILDER PLACE YEAR	OTHER DETAILS
BRAVO (2)	1798 760	297.0 42.3 17.2	H. Robb Ltd. Leith 1947	Sold 4.7.1966, to Fairtide Ltd. Rochester, and Malta. Renamed *CONSTANTINE*. Sold 1969, for scrapping at Spain. Arrived Bilbao 14.7.1969.
CARLO (3)	1799 757	297.0 42.3 17.3	Hall Russell Aberdeen 1947	Sold 25.7.1966, to Chr. M. Sarlis, Patras. Renamed *PELASGOS*. Sold 16.10.1972, renamed *SITHIRO SCRAP,* for scrapping in Greece.
DAGO (2)	2302 966	309.0 46.2 19.7	Ailsa SB Co. Troon 1947	Sold 25.5.1962, to South African Coasters (Prty) Durban. Renamed *VERGE*. Sold 1969, renamed *SONRISA* (Monrovia). Sold 1971, for scrapping in Pakistan, arrived Karachi 18.2.1971.
DOMINO (4)	2302 966	309.0 46.2 19.7	Ailsa SB Co. Troon 1947	Sold 28.8.1962, to South African Coasters (prty) Durban. Renamed *RIDGE*. Sold 1969, renamed *NOBLEZA* (Monrovia). Sold 1971, for scrapping in Pakistan, arrived Karachi 26.2.1971.
LEO (3)	1792 712	296.10 42-2 17.2	Swan Hunter & Wigham Richardson Newcastle 1947	Sold 25.10.1967, to Malta Maritime Services. Renamed *MALCOLM PACE*. Sold 1970, renamed *OLES* (Malta). Sold 1974, renamed *MARSA* (Malta). Sold 1979, for scrapping at Catania, Italy.
MARENGO (3)	4981 2555	419.7 55.10 25.6	Swan Hunter & Wigham Richardson Newcastle, 1947	Sold 20.10.1967, to Inomaen Cia Nav. SA, Panama. Renamed *NEA MONI* (Greek). Laid up at Piraeus from 2.4.1971. Sold 1972, for scrapping in Turkey. Arrived Yalava 22.7.1972.
SILVIO (3)	1798 760	297.0 42.3 17.2	Henry Robb Ltd. Leith 1947	Sold 28.10.1966, to Malta Maritime Services. Renamed *KRISTINE PACE*. Damaged by fire 5.9.1969, at Valetta and subsequently sold for scrapping at Spezia.
TINTO (2)	1795 757	297.0 42.2 17.2	Henry Robb Ltd. Leith 1947	Sold 31.5.1966, to Mann Greenfield Ltd., Gibraltar. Renamed *KATE M.G.* 1966, renamed *BOGOTA* 1967, renamed *HOPI* 1967, renamed *BOGOTA* 1968, renamed *VICTORIA*. Sold 1968 to Santa Domingo owner. Damaged 20.6.1969. Out of class 28.11.1969. 6.1971, reported as lying at Santa Maria, Columbia. Appears to have been scrapped unrepaired prior to 5.1978.
TRURO (3)	1795 757	297.0 42.3 17.2	Henry Robb Ltd. Leith 1947	Sold 23.5.1968, to W. J. Towell & Co. Kuwait. Renamed *GULF NOOR*. Sold 1971. Renamed *GULF PROSPERITY* (Panama). Sold 1972, for scrapping in Pakistan, arrived at Karachi 28.5.1972.

NAME FORMER NAMES	GROSS NET	LENGTH BREADTH DEPTH	BUILDER PLACE YEAR	OTHER DETAILS
RIALTO (2)	5005 2585	419.7 55.10 25.6	Swan Hunter & Wigham Richardson Newcastle, 1949	Sold 17.6.1970, to Tiara Shipping Co. Famagusta. Renamed *SANDRA*. Sold 5.1971, for scrapping at Whampoa, China.
BORODINO (3)	3206 1798	312.1 48.8 17.11	Ailsa SB Co. Troon 1950	Sold 26.7.1967, to Van Heyghen Freres, for scrapping at Ghent.
CAVALLO (3) m.v.	2340 1251	309.7 48.8 19.5	Henry Robb Ltd. Leith 1951	Sold 6.7.1971, to Maldive Shipping Co. Male. Renamed *MALDIVE VENTURE*. Sold 1980, for scrapping in India, arrived Calcutta 23.8.1980.
TRENTINO (2) m.v.	2340 1251	309.7 48.8 19.5	Henry Robb Ltd. Leith 1952	Sold 6.7.1971, to Maldive Shipping Co. Male. Renamed *MALDIVE ENSIGN*. Sold 5.1980, for scrapping at Kauhsiung, Taiwan. Left Hong Kong 8.5.1980.
CICERO (2)	2497 1028	309.8 48.8 17.10	Henry Robb Ltd Leith 1954	Sold 2.10.1970, to Maldive Shipping Co. Male. Renamed *MALDIVE BUILDER*. Sold 1977, for scrapping in Pakistan, arrived Gadani Beach 30.6.1977.
ROLLO (3)	2530 1028	309.8 48.8 17.10	Henry Robb Ltd Leith 1954	Sold 29.6.1971, to Maldive Shipping Co. Male. Renamed *OCEAN EMPRESS*. Sold 1977, for scrapping in Pakistan, arrived Gadani Beach 27.9.1977.
TEANO (3)	1580 595	277.2 43.1 16.11	Henry Robb Ltd Leith 1955	Sold 29.10.1968, to Maldive Shipping Co. Male. Renamed *ASIONE*. 1969, renamed *OCEAN DUCHESS*. Beached 13.6.1976, at Bahrain after fire in engine room. Sold 1977, for scrapping at Pakistan, arrived Gadani Beach 8.3.1977.
AARO (2) m.v.	2468 1262	330.3 48.11 19.4	Henry Robb Ltd Leith 1960	Sold 11.5.1972, to Maldive Shipping Co. Male. Renamed *MALDIVE TRUST*. Sold 1981, renamed *ISLAMI* (Kuwait). Sold 1983, renamed *MALDIVE FAITH* (Male). Sold 1984, renamed *NORTHERN STAR* (Male). Sold 1986, for scrapping at Pakistan arrived Gadani Beach 18.9.1986.
RAPALLO m.v.	3402 1453	365.10 54.5 21.0	Henry Robb Ltd Leith 1960	In 1968, the *RAPALLO* under command of Captain F. Meetham performed one of the finest feats of deep-sea towage in modern history towing the Harrison Line's *TACTITION* (which had suffered an engine room fire) over 1,000 miles to the Azores. The tow took two weeks arriving at Porta Delgada on 4.7.1968. Transferred 3.4.1973, to Ellerman City Lines. 1975, renamed *CITY OF LIMASSOL*. Sold 1977, renamed *BEITEDDINE* (Lebonese). Sold 1986, for scrapping in Spain. Arrived Aviles 14.7.1986.

mv. *RAPALLO* 1960-1973

ENGINE:	oil 2SA 7 cyl. Sulzer.
MADE BY:	G. Clark & N.E. Marine Ltd. Sunderland.
POWER:	3500 BHP
SPEED:	13½ knots
SERVICE:	North America.
PASSENGERS:	12 — 1st Class.

Photograph courtesy of Fotoflite.

mv. *SALERNO (5)* 1965-1973

ENGINE:	oil 4 SA 6 cyl.
MADE BY:	Mirrlees National Ltd. Stockport.
POWER:	2580 BHP
SPEED:	14 knots
SERVICE:	Scandinavia, Mediterranean.
PASSENGERS:	Nil.

Ltd as agents in Hull for the service.

In the meantime, prior to the latter part of 1966, the *Rialto*, which had returned to the service, and the *Rinaldo*, a steamer of 2,957 tons, built in 1946, had replaced the *Arcadian* and the *Bassano*. Under the Wilson flag, the *Rialto* completed her last trip on August 25, 1966, the *Rapallo* hers on October 9, the *Rinaldo* hers on November 3, and the *Marengo* hers on December 6, 1966. The last sailing of all by the Wilson Line was taken by mv *Rathlin Head*, on charter, leaving Hull on February 9, 1967, all subsequent sailings being under the Cairn flag using mainly chartered British ships. Three of the five Wilson Line vessels which had latterly been concerned in this trade were disposed of during 1967. The *Rinaldo* was sold to the Greek firm United Maritime Lines Corporation and renamed *Emerald*, being resold in 1968 to the Union Commercial Shipping Company, also Greek. The *Bassano* was sold to the Greaksea Shipping Company S/A (Greece) and renamed *Athanasia*, while the Channel Islands. Originally having the name *Williamstown*, she was bought by the Wilson Line and renamed in 1946. Throughout she served on the Antwerp run until making her last sailing from London on June 6, 1967. She was sold in the same year to D. G. Gaetanos and others (of Greece, of course!) and renamed *Georgis*. Her successor on the Antwerp service was mv *Norfolk Trader*, on long-term charter from the Great Yarmouth Shipping Co Ltd. She was built in 1954 as the *Arbon* and changed hands in 1956; her gross tonnage is 457.

Now to the Mediterranean, an area of trade in which the Wilson Line has a very old-established interest (though it never attained the high importance attached to the Scandinavian area). It will be noticed that in the above fleet disposition plan only chartered shipping is in use. During the period under review, few of Wilson's own ships have been used on their own services, yet their vessels which had previously operated there, like the motor-ships *Trentino*

A more recent addition, in 1960, for the Canadian route was the motor-ship *Rapallo*.

[*Courtesy: Ellerman's Wilson Line Ltd.*

mv. *SPERO (3)* 1966-1973

ENGINE: 4 oil 4 SA 6 cyl.
MADE BY: Mirrlees National
             Ltd. Stockport.
POWER: 10,920 BHP
SPEED: 18 knots
SERVICE: Gothenburg.
PASSENGERS: 408 — One Class.

mv. *DESTRO (3)* 1970-1978

ENGINE: 2 oil 4 SA each 8 cyl.
MADE BY: Lindholmens Varv.
             A/B, Gothenburg.
POWER: 7999 BHP
SPEED: 14 knots
SERVICE: Scandinavia.
PASSENGERS: Nil.

NAME FORMER NAMES	GROSS NET	LENGTH BREADTH DEPTH	BUILDER PLACE YEAR	OTHER DETAILS
SALERNO (5) *m.v.*	1559 703	307.9 45.8 16.8	Henry Robb Ltd Leith 1965	Transferred 9.1.1973, to Ellerman City Lines. 1975, renamed *CITY OF CORINTH*. Sold 1978, renamed *PYCROS STAR* (Liberia). Sold 1981, renamed *PAXI* (Cyprus). Sold 1986, renamed *LEFKAS SUN* (Honduras). Sold 1988, renamed *GENIKI* (Malaysia). Still in service.
SPERO (3) *m.v.*	6916 3403	454.4 68.2 17.6	Cammell Laird Ltd. Birkenhead 1966	Sold 1.5.1973, to Maritime Company, Lesvos. Renamed *SAPPHO*. Still in service.
SALMO (3) *m.v.*	1523 708	308.0 45.8 16.8	Henry Robb Ltd Leith 1967	Transferred 9.1.1973, to Ellerman City Lines. 1974, renamed *CITY OF ATHENS*. Sold 1977, renamed *ALDEBAREN 11* (Panama). Sold 1980, renamed *ARGIMO* (Cyprus). Sold 1987, renamed *AL AMEEN* (St. Vincent). Sold 1988, for scrapping at Pakistan, arrived Gadani Beach 23.1.1988.
SORRENTO (3) *m.v.*	1523 708	308.0 45.8 16.8	Henry Robb Ltd Leith 1967	Transferred 9.1.1973, to Ellerman City Lines. 1974, renamed *CITY OF OF SPARTA*. Sold 1977, renamed *GRACECHURCH* (British). Sold 1983, renamed *WAYBRIDGE* (Gibraltar). Sold 1986, renamed *FIVE STARS* (St. Vincent). Still in service.
ANGELO (3) m.v. x *BYLAND* *ABBEY*	1372 552	265.4 40.6 14.6	Austin & Pickersgill Sunderland 1957	Bought 13.2.1968, from Associated Humber Lines. Renamed *ANGELO*. Sold 1970, Maldive Shipping Co. Male. Renamed *MALDIVE EXPORTER*. Sold 1980, for scrapping in Pakistan, arrived Gadani Beach 15.12.1980.
ARIOSTO (5) m.v. x *KIRKHAM* *ABBEY*	1372 553	265.4 40.6 14.6	Austin & Pickersgill Sunderland 1956	Bought 13.2.1968, from Associated Humber Lines. Renamed *ARIOSTO*. Sold 1970, Maldive Shipping Co. Male. Renamed *MALDIVE IMPORTER*. Sold 1983, for scrapping in Pakistan, arrived Gadani Beach 9.8.1983.
SANGRO m.v.	1523 708	308.0 45.8 16.8	Henry Robb Ltd Leith 1968	Transferred 9.1.1973, to Ellerman City Lines. 1974, renamed *CITY OF ANKARA*. Sold 1978, renamed *REZEKI* (Singapore). Sold 1988, renamed *MELINA* (Indonesia). Still in service.
SILVIO (4) m.v.	1523 708	308.0 45.8 16.8	Henry Robb Ltd Leith 1968	Transferred 9.1.1973, to Ellerman City Lines. 1974, renamed *CITY OF PATRAS*. Sold 1978, renamed *CITY OF TEMA* (Ghana) Sold 1987, renamed *LEMISSIA* (Cyprus). Sold 1988, renamed *SHAZLI* (St. Vincent). Sold 1990, renamed *AMITY*, (St. Vincent). Still in service.

NAME FORMER NAMES	GROSS NET	LENGTH BREADTH DEPTH	BUILDER PLACE YEAR	OTHER DETAILS
DESTRO (3) m.v.	1599 590	360.0 63.1 16.3	Ankerlokken Verft Frederikstad 1970	Sold 1.12.1978, to Ignazio Messina, Genoa. Renamed *JOLLY AZZURRO*. 1982 renamed *JOLLY CELESTE*. Sold 1990, renamed *PRESLAW* (Belgium). Still in service.
DOMINO (5) m.v.	1582 590	356.0 63.4 16.1	Langvik MV. Sarpsbirg 1972	Sold 4.12.1978, to Ignazioi Messina, Genoa. Renamed *JOLLY NERO*. Sold 1990, renamed *SERDICA* (Bulgarian). Still in service.
HERO (4) m.v.	3468 1071	375.9 63.4 19.2	Robb Caledon SB Ltd. Leith, 1972	Capsized 13.11.1977, after developing a list during force 10 gale, in the North Sea 50 miles N.W. of Heligoland. 1 crewman was lost.

ELLERMAN LINES

NAME FORMER NAMES	GROSS NET	LENGTH BREADTH DEPTH	BUILDER PLACE YEAR	OTHER DETAILS
CICERO (3) m.v.	11,922 7,132	147.17m 22.53 6.86	Smith's Dock Co. Ltd. Middlesbrough 1978	7.5.1981, Register transferred to Georgetown, Cayman Islands. Sold 1988, to Clarke Transport, St. Johns Newfoundland, retained name. Still in service.
CAVALLO (4) m.v.	11,922 7,132	147.17m 22.53 6.86	Smith's Dock Co. Ltd. Middlesbrough 1979	1981, Register transferred to Newcastle, N.B. Canada. Sold 1988, to Clarke Transport, St. Johns, Newfoundland, renamed *CABOT*. Still in service.

The majority of the Ellerman's Wilson Line postwar fleet, were equipped to carry 12 passengers in considerable style and comfort. Classed as passenger cargo liners they were fully booked, year in year out.

The cruises varied from 10 days to Norway, Denmark and Gothenburg, 21 days to Stockholm and east Sweden, 4-5 weeks to the Mediterranean. The ships were patronised by personalities from stage, screen and television. There was a good mix of professional and business people as well as writers and journalists.

A cruise on a "Wilson Line" passenger cargo liner, offered excellent food and drink, sea air, interesting ports of call, stimulating conversation and relaxation in fine public rooms or in a deck chair.

*The passenger lounge of the **Borodino** in 1953. This vessel carried 36 passengers and worked on the Hull – Copenhagen service.*

The passenger lounge of the **Cavallo** *in 1951.*

The passenger lounge of the **Cicero** *in 1954.*

The Dining Saloon of the **Cicero** *in 1954.*

A stateroom on the **Cicero** *in 1954.*

*Popular entertainers Wilfred and Mable Pickles (right) are among the passengers of the **Borodino** on 29th July 1955. (left) Ch. Officer R. Whittleton and his wife Audrey.*

*The crew of the **Borodino** and their families enjoy a social evening at the City Hotel circa 1953.*

LIST OF VESSELS LOST DUE TO ENEMY ACTION DURING THE 1914 — 1918 WAR.

NAME	BUILT *ACQUIRED	DATE SUNK	HOW SUNK	CASUALTIES
RUNO (1)	1902	05.09.1914	Mined	29
TRURO (1)	1898	06.05.1915	Torpedoed	Nil
GUIDO (1)	1913	08.07.1915	Torpedoed	Nil
GRODNO (2)	1912	12.08.1915	Torpedoed	Nil
SERBINO	1913	16.08.1915	Torpedoed	Nil
URBINO (3)	1915	24.09.1915	Torpedoed	Nil
SALERNO (3)	1912	14.10.1015	Mined	Nil
COLENSO	1900	30.11.1915	Gunfire	1
DIDO (2)	1896	24.02.1916	Mined	28
TEANO (1)	1913	29.06.1916	Scuttled	Nil
CALYPSO (2)	1904	10.07.1916	Torpedoed	30
AARO (1)	1909	01.08.1916	Torpedoed	3
THURSO (2)	1909	27.09.1916	Gunfire	Nil
SPERO (1)	1896	02.11.1916	Torpedoed	Nil
VASCO (1)	1895	16.11.1916	Mined	17
CANNIZARO	1914	28.03.1917	Torpedoed	Nil
SALMO (1)	1900	07.04.1917	Torpedoed	2
TORO	1904	12.04.1917	Torpedoed	14
ZARA	*1903	13.04.1917	Torpedoed	27
RINALDO (2)	1908	18.04.1917	Torpedoed	Nil
CITO (1)	1899	17.05.1917	Gunfire	11
TYCHO	1904	20.05.1917	Torpedoed	15
OSWEGO	1916	29.05.1917	Torpedoed	Nil
BUFFALO (2)	1907	18.06.1917	Torpedoed	Nil
KELSO (2)	1909	19.06.1917	Torpedoed	Nil
CATTARO (1)	1912	26.06.1917	Torpedoed	Nil
TORCELLO (1)	1912	15.07.1917	Torpedoed	1
OSLO	1905	21.08.1917	Torpedoed	3
HIDALGO (2)	1908	28.08.1917	Torpedoed	15
ERATO (2)	1911	01.09.1917	Mined	Nil
COLORADO (2)	1914	20.10.1917	Torpedoed	4
CARLO (1)	1913	13.11.1917	Torpedoed	2
KYNO (1)	1913	16.11.1917	Torpedoed	5
CAVALLO (1)	1913	01.02.1918	Torpedoed	3
JAFFA	*1903	02.02.1918	Torpedoed	10
POLO (2)	1913	12.02.1918	Torpedoed	3
ROMEO	1881	03.03.1918	Torpedoed	29
DESTRO (1)	1914	25.03.1918	Torpedoed	Nil
CICERO (1)	1895	10.04.1918	Scuttled	Nil
MONTEBELLO (2)	1911	21.06.1918	Torpedoed	41
CHICAGO (3)	1917	08.07.1918	Torpedoed	3

LIST OF THE COMPANY'S SHIPS TAKEN OVER DURING THE GREAT WAR 1914 — 1918.

NAME	BUILT	DETAILS
BORODINO (1)	1911	August 1914. Chartered to the Royal Navy as a depot ship, anchored at Scapa Flow. Returned to Wilson's in 1919.
GOURKO	1911	August 1914. Chartered to the Royal Navy used as a Theatre ship, for the Grand Fleet at Scapa Flow.
ARGYLE	1872	September 1914. Sold to the British Government and sunk as a block ship at Scapa Flow.
LORNE	1873	October 1914. Sold to the British Government and sunk as a block ship at Scapa flow.
CLIO (2)	1889	November 1914. Sold to the British Government and sunk as a block ship at Scapa Flow.
RONDA	1889	January 1915. Sold to the British Government and sunk as a block ship at Scapa Flow.
CASTRO (2)	1911	August 1914. Detained at Hamburg, before the declaration of war. Taken over by the German Navy, renamed *LIBAU*. Scuttled to avoid capture, 22nd April 1916.
HULL	1907	August 1914. Detained at Hamburg, before the declaration of war. Interned for the duration and returned to her owners 28th February 1919.
ESKIMO	1910	9th December 1914. Taken over by the Royal Navy as an Armed Merchant Cruiser. Captured by the German Navy off Risor in July 1916. Returned on 19.1.1919.

BUILT in 1904 by Earle's Shipbuilding and Engineering Co. at Hull, the ss. *Tycho*'s dimensions were: Length, 335ft, breadth 47ft, depth 22ft 9in. Gross tons, 3,216; net tons, 2,029.

The *Tycho* was sunk after being torpedoed off Beachy Head on May 20 1917. The accompanying report on the circumstances of the sinking was submitted by her chief officer, E. R. Massam.

Dated Hull 22nd May, 1917, the report is addressed to Commander H. L. Walton, RNR, Ellerman's Wilson Line Ltd. Hull.

Dear Sir

S.S. "TYCHO"

I regret to report the sinking of the above ship under the following circumstances. We passed Owers L. Vessel, bound for Hull, about 4.27 p.m. G.M.T. May 20th, weather: light S.E. wind, sea smooth, hazy with rain at intervals. At 6.5 p.m. the ship was struck, presumably with a torpedo, on the starboard side of No.2 hatch, no submarine being visible at the time. The engines were stopped, as the vessel was rapidly sinking, and all hands mustered at the boats, which were then lowered into the water. All the crew then left the ship, Captain Williams being the last man to leave, and before doing so he destroyed all his confidential documents, the vessel finally sinking about half-an-hour after being struck. The ss. "Porthkerry" which was about a quarter of a mile away, turned round to pick up our boats both of which got safely alongside her. A torpedo was then seen coming towards the "Porthkerry", and before any steps could be taken to avoid it the torpedo struck the ship and Captain Williams' boat at the same time, shattering the boat and killing all the crew, except one man who was eventually picked up. My boat was at the same time capsized, and we were thrown into the water, the ss "Porthkerry" sinking in about two minutes after being struck, and seven of her crew were drowned. Before sinking, the "Porthkerry" managed to get one boat away, and this boat under the command of the Chief Engineer, (the Senior surviving Officer) picked us up, having great difficulty owing to the large amount of wreckage, after we had been in the water about half an hour. Later the s.s. "Esperante" of London picked us up and took us into Newhaven.

I cannot speak too highly of the behaviour of all our crew. Mr. Pearson, the third Officer, is especially deserving of mention as he not only kept 14 men together hanging on to the keel of the upturned lifeboat but actually rescued the cook and a seaman from beneath the capsized boat.

Yours truly,
(signed) E. R. Massam,
Chief Officer

THE ss. "CITO"

Copy
CONFIDENTIAL

HULL
21st May 1917

Commander H. L. Walton, R.N.R.,
      Marine Superintendent,
            Ellerman's Wilson Line, Ld.,
                  Hull.

Dear Sir,

S/S "CITO"

I regret to report the loss of the above vessel under the following circumstances:-

We left Hull on the 12th May for Rotterdam, and proceeded according to instructions to Yarmouth Roads, leaving this latter place 3.20 p.m. on the 17th., C.M.T., proceeding according to Admiralty instructions under escort. I was off duty from 8.0 to 12.0 p.m., and at 11.45 p.m. on the 17th. was awakened by gun fire. On going on deck I found we were in a dense fog, and an enemy destroyer on each quarter. less than 100 yards distant, shelling the ship. I went up to the boat deck, and found the port boat shot away. I ordered two men who were in the vicinity to stand by the starboard boat, and then tried to get forward, but found the way blocked by wreckage. There were also several injured or dead men lying on deck, but in the dark and fog I could not ascertain who they were. During this time the enemy vessels continued to fire practically at point-blank range, and the ship was rapidly sinking. The Captain then called to me from the bridge to get the boat away, which I immediately proceeded to do, having got nine of the crew into the boat. We just managed to get the boat clear when the ship turned over on her side and sank, one destroyer firing at her right up to the last. When the boat got clear of the ship we narrowly escaped being rammed by one of the destroyers. I cruised about in the vicinity for about three hours, but did not hear or see anything of the remainder of the crew, the weather still being calm and foggy. About 3.0 a.m. a light breeze sprang up, and we set sail and set a course for the English Coast, where we arrived safely at 8.30 p.m. on the 18th May, and were picked up by a drifter and taken into Lowestoft.

When Captain Orme was calling out his orders to me, his voice appeared calm and collected, and the behaviour of the crew was splendid under most trying conditions.

Yours truly
(signed) George Chapman
Chief Officer.

ss. *URBINO*

Kapitan-Leutnant Hanson in U41 was fresh out of Wilhelmshaven and on Sept. 23 1915 he first came up with the horse-transport "Anglo Colombian", sank her by gunfire, then quickly caught the Harrison Line's "Chancellor", dispatched her in the same way and took his third ship, the Houston vessel "Hesione" — 86 miles south by east of the Fastnet. She too was sunk by gunfire.

The next day she sank her fourth victim "Urbino". Then the famous "Q" — ship "Baralong" of Bucknall line commanded by Lieut-Commander Godfrey Herbert turned up on the scene.

U-41 attempted the same technique of capture and sink by gunfire only to find too late that this one had guns as well and suffered the fate of her former victims. Only Hanson and one man were picked up and Hanson died later.

LIST OF VESSELS LOST DUE TO ENEMY ACTION DURING THE 1939 — 1945 WAR.

NAME	BUILT *ACQUIRED	DATE SUNK	HOW SUNK	CASUALTIES
TRURO (2)	1922	15.09.1939	Torpedoed	Nil
ALBANO (2)	1912	02.03.1940	Mined	9
SALERNO (4)	1924	02.05.1940	Captured	Nil
SALMO (2)	1924	03.07.1940	Captured	Nil
LEO (2)	*1920	25.07.1940	Bombed	6
KYNO (2)	1924	28.08.1940	Torpedoed	5
TASSO (4)	1938	02.12.1940	Torpedoed	5
SILVIO (2)	1913	21.12.1940	Bombed	2
BASSANO (3)	1937	09.01.1941	Torpedoed	1
DRACO (2)	1922	11.04.1941	Bombed	1
CAVALLO (2)	1922	25.04.1941	Bombed	Nil
DOMINO (3)	1925	03.05.1941	Bombed	Nil
TRENTINO (1)	1919	08.05.1941	Bombed	Nil
ERATO (3)	1923	28.07.1941	Torpedoed	9
ARIOSTO (3)	1940	24.10.1941	Torpedoed	6
VOLO (2)	1938	28.12.1941	Torpedoed	24
DAGO (1)	1902	15.03.1942	Bombed	Nil
THURSO (3)	1919	15.06.1942	Torpedoed	13
KELSO (3)	1924	08.08.1942	Torpedoed	3
CITY OF RIPON	1915	11.11.1942	Torpedoed	56
GUIDO (2)	1920	08.03.1943	Torpedoed	10
RUNO (2)	1920	11.04.1943	Torpedoed	16
DYNAMO (2)	1920	17.04.1943	Mined	7

LIST OF VESSELS BOUGHT BY THE ADMIRALTY

NAME	BUILT *ACQUIRED	DATE SUNK	HOW SUNK	CASUALTIES
CARLO (2)	*1920	09.1939	Ammunition Hulk	
MOURINO (2)	1906	09.1939	Ammunition Hulk	
BORODINO (2)	1911	26.09.1939	Sunk as a Blockship	
GOURKO (2)	1911	21.05.1940	Sunk as a Blockship	

(Insurance Department).

10th February 1943.

ss. "CITY OF RIPON"

On passage from Capetown to New York via Trinidad.

Captain Robinson states:-

On the 11th November 1942, approximate position 8.20 N. 59.40 W. speed about 10 knots, not in convoy, vessel attacked by two submarines. The vessel was first hit by a torpedo on the port side, after part of the engine room, at 3.21 a.m., engines immediately disabled and orders given to abandon ship. Three lifeboats and three rafts safely launched, but whilst alongside on the starboard side two more torpedoes struck the vessel amidships and blew one lifeboat to pieces. Another lifeboat capsized through the explosions. The lifeboat which was blown to pieces had about 40 men in it, but only 2 were eventually picked up out of the water. The Chief Steward was alone in the remaining lifeboat until a Wireless Operator swam to it and climbed on board; then the Master left the vessel and swam to the same boat. These 3 men then picked up 24 of the crew out of the water, therefore only 27 men were saved in all out of a total crew of 83.

"CITY OF RIPON " sank about 3.26 a.m. on the 11th November.

The lifeboat crew were picked up by the Brazilian vessel "MIDOSI" at 11 a.m. on the 12th November and landed at Trinidad on the 14th November.

All the confidential papers, including the ship's Register, went down with the vessel.

s.s. "TASSO"

On voyage from West Indies to Hull (diversion)

Captain Scarbrough states:

At 5.15 a.m. Monday 2nd December 1940 position 320 miles West of Ireland the vessel was struck by a torpedo. She was the third vessel in the outside Port Column, speed 9 knots, and at the time of torpedoing on an independent zig zag course 20° to 100°. This had been previously arranged in case of trouble.

The explosion occurred in the vicinity of the magazine starboard quarter immediately putting the stern right under up to the alleyway doors. The bridge caved in, numbers 3 and 4 hatches and coamings blew off, bulkheads collapsed and starboard lifeboat completely destroyed. There were several vessels sinking in the vicinity but the Captain thinks he saw the "TASSO" disappear about three quarters of an hour after explosion.

Most of the survivors got away from the vessel in the port lifeboats others jumping into the water, of which some were picked up by the lifeboat. Five lives were lost including the Chief Engineer who was killed by the explosion.

The survivors were in the lifeboat three hours before being picked up by H.M.S. "VISCOUNT", a destroyer, this vessel being one of the escort which was to meet the convoy the next morning.

The escort vessel at the time of the attack was the armed cruiser "FORFAR", this vessel being the first to be sunk with large loss of life. At least seven other vessels were sunk in the attack, which was made by several submarines.

All confidential papers went down with the vessel.

s.s. "DOMINO"

Steamer completed bunkering about 8 p.m. on Saturday — 3rd May — and was moved across the dock alongside the shed to lay until time for sailing.

The air-raid commenced at about 10.30 p.m. I was ashore and unable to return to the ship owing to the heavy "blitz" which soon developed.

According to the Chief Officer, who was on board with twenty members of the Crew, showers of incendiaries fell on the ship, which the ship's fire-fighting squad were able to extinguish, but the shed quickly became ablaze, and despite the efforts of part of the crew who dashed into the shed, it continued to burn fiercely. During this time many more incendiaries and high-explosives were dropping all round.

The wind at this time was blowing the ship on the quay. Later, however, the wind changed and the flames swept over the steamer. The crew cast off the moorings in the hope that the ship would drift away from the blazing shed, but before this could be achieved, the shed walls collapsed and fell on her, immediately setting the vessel afire fore and aft.

By now the ship's fire appliances were all burnt, and when she had drifted to the other side of the Dock, the shore Fire Brigade took over, but it was impossible for them to get the fires under control as all the super structure and holds were blazing furiously. The Fire Brigade advised the Crew to abanadon the ship, which was effected without any casualties, and the former continued to work until Sunday afternoon, when it was found impossible to do anything further and the vessel was pushed across the other side of the Dock alongside the burnt-out shed.

I was able to get down to the Dock by Noon on Sunday but could not assist in any way, beyond advising the Fire Brigade to watch the possibility of the steamer capsizing, in view of the amount of water which was being pumped into the vessel.

On Monday morning the ship turned on her starboard side and capsized.

signed   J. E. Stott
Master

LIVERPOOL
6th May 1941.

ss. *HULL*

The Wilson's & North Eastern Railway Shipping Company steamer *Hull*, ran aground at about 11 pm on 18th October 1908. At Dimlington opposite Slated Farm,1 mile north of Easington. The *Presto* and other tugs made several attempts to refloat her but she remained fast.

Acting on the advice of local seafarers some cargo was jettisoned and the *Hull* was refloated at 3 am on 23rd October. The *Hull* then proceeded to the port of Hull where the rest of her cargo was discharged. The *Hull* then entered dry-dock for repairs.

RMS *BAYARDO*

The *Bayardo* left Gothenburg on 19th January 1912, with a crew of 44, 42 passengers and 1800 tons of general cargo, it was her 13th voyage. On her passage across the North Sea the *Bayardo* encountered fog. On 21st October, as the *Bayardo* approached the Humber estuary the fog became dense, she proceeded with caution up the river towards Hull. To check the depth of water in the narrow channel regular soundings were taken, however at about 7 am the *Bayardo* ran aground on the Middle Sand opposite Alexandra dock. Due to the seriousness of the situation the passengers were taken off in the ship's three lifeboats then transferred to the tug *Presto*. Despite attempts by tugs to refloat her the stricken ship remained fast and when the tide receded the strain broke her back.

It was soon realised the *BAYARDO* was doomed and no course of action could refloat her. It was decided to strip the wreck of any valuable fittings and this work was carried out by joiners from the Earle's shipyard from which the *Bayardo* had been launched the previous July. Also a large amount of cargo was recovered by about a hundred labourers loading into five lighters as tidal conditions permitted.

But with each tide the wreck sank lower and filled with sand and mud. Soon the once elegant liner had to be left to her fate, being dispersed by explosives.

ss.*SAPPHO*

The crew of the *Sappho* were looking forward to spending Christmas with their families when they left the Russian port of Archangel on 28th November 1915, bound for Hull with a cargo of pit props. But the ship became stuck in ice and despite efforts to break free by continuously dropping the anchor no progress was made.

By Christmas Eve provisions were down to a week's supply and the *Sappho* was held in ice nine feet thick. The crew had become increasingly impatient and as the weather was clear Captain Martin decided the crew should abandon ship and attempt to walk 18 miles across the ice floes to the lightship at Cross Island. The crew set off wrapped in blankets but otherwise wearing only ordinary clothes and sailors' boots. The scarce provisions were put in packs.

Only two hours headway was made on the first day on the ice and camp was made on a large ice floe. But the young members of the crew walked about until the party set off again as they feared if they sat down they would freeze to death. On Christmas Day the crew's ordeal became more difficult because the compass they had been navigating by froze in temperatures of 40 degrees below zero. By Boxing Day, the Master and Chief Engineer who had been helped along for most of the journey became too exhausted to continue, the steward volunteered to stay and look after them along with a 16 year old seaman, they were never seen again.

The party which pressed on was led by Finnish seaman Martin Hautica who walked in front testing the ice with a boat hook. During Boxing Day, 11 young members of the crew who thought the others were slowing them down made the fatal decision to forge ahead on their own. Nothing was heard of 10 of them and the 11th man the cook was later found suffering from frostbite, he eventually had to be left behind. Two members of the crew unable to carry on, were left to their fate on the same night. Next to be left was the Mate and Second Engineer who had become delirious and thought they were back on the *Sappho*. Only three crew were left and when 17 year old Jack Stork fell through the ice he was saved from drowning by the Second Mate. The three reached land the next day and followed telegraph posts until they met a Laplander with a sleigh who took the survivors to the village of Sosnovetz, where they were fed and warmed.

The men returned to England on 26th February 1916, ending one of the many tragic episodes in Hull's maritime history.

The *Sappho* was found in January 1816 by the icebreaker *Sadko* about halfway between the islands of Daniloff and Morshovetz about 10 miles off the mainland. The icebreaker could not get near her but a party was sent on board.

The Hammerfest sealer Alfred Edward found the *Sappho* drifting in the White Sea, 30 miles north of Cape Kanin and took her in tow. The fore hold and engine room were full of water so with the assistance of pumps an attempt was made to keep the *Sappho* afloat and tow her to the nearest harbour. Despite two days of hard work towing, pumping with two hoses and buckets the *Sappho* foundered on 16th May 1916, owing to a heavy N.W. swell which commenced on the last day. The seas having risen over the greater part of the cargo in the forehold.

ss. *VASCO*

On 12th December 1948 the *Vasco* was on passage from Hull to Barry, South Wales bound for the Mediterranean, when she was holed after striking a submerged object outside the Spurn. The Captain acting on the advice of the river pilot, beached the sinking vessel at Haile Sand, in the Humber estuary. Pumps and repair equipment was taken out to the *Vasco* by several local tugs.

On 7th January 1949, the *Vasco* was refloated and with the tugs *Presto, Airman, Rifleman, Yorkshireman* and *Pinky* in attendance was beached in a better more sheltered position off Cleethorpes. On 10th January, the *Vasco* raised steam and with her attendant tugs safely arrived at Immingham for dry-docking and repairs.

ss. VOLO

The *Volo* was badly damaged by fire whilst berthed at Gothenburg, on 4th November 1960. The fire which started in number two hold, in a cargo of wood wool, during the afternoon burned for over 24 hours. A Swedish firefighter was hurt whilst burning a hole in the after deck to gain access to fight the fire from further aft. There must have been a build up of gas for he was blown over the handrail and onto the quay.

Eventually the fire was extinguished and the *Volo* was taken to the repair yard for an extensive refit. The *Volo* sailed from Gothenburg in early February 1961 and went onto the Stockholm trade.

mv. HERO

On 12th November 1977, the ro-ro ferry *Hero* was on passage across the North Sea from Grimsby to Esbjerg in a force 10 gale, when she developed a severe list. This was due to sea water entering the vessel through the stern and flooding the trailer deck and engine room, at a rate faster than the ship's pumps could cope with.

A May-day was sent out at 10.40 a.m. which was responded to by several ships in the vicinity and the coastguards. Of the ships complement of 27 crew and 3 passengers, 11 were lifted off by a German Sea King helicopter, and landed on the *Tor Britannia*. The rest abandoned the *Hero* into two life-rafts, and were picked up by the Grimsby vessel *Valerie* and a helicopter from the Canadian frigate *Huron*. Unfortunately one crewman was lost.

The *Hero* foundered the next day.

*The ss. **Como** navigating the River Avon near Bristol.*
*Between 1925-1930 the **Como** was transferred to*
Ellerman Papayanni Line,
for use on their continental service.
*During the 1939-1945 War the **Como** survived*
sailing in the two convoys which resulted in
*the loss of the **Ariosto** and the **Erato**. She ended*
the war as a boom defence vessel at Yarmouth.
Photograph: by courtesy of Mrs. Lowish.

*The Ellerman's Wilson Line tugs **Presto** and*
***Forto** manoeuvring off King George Dock,*
*Hull, with their charge the ss. **Marengo**,*
which has just arrived from North America,
via Aberdeen.
The two tugs were sold out of the fleet in
1968, at a time when most of the old steam
ships had been sold and replaced by modern
vessels which could usually operate without
tugs.

*The ss. **Palermo** laying at the "Pool of London" loading cargo from wharf and river craft circa 1963,
whilst on passage from Hull and London to Greece, Cyprus and Turkey. The "Pool of London" is the farthest point
that ocean going vessels can navigate up the River Thames.*

The ss. **Bravo** *berthed at Albert Dock, Hull, loading for Swedish ports, is receiving an 83 ton roll of steel from the port's heavy lift floating crane barge. The* **Bravo** *and her sister ships were affectionately known as "Green Parrots" by ship enthusiasts because of their colourful livery.*

The ss. **Volo** *at the "Wilson Line" berth on the main Quay at Gothenburg. The company had long historic trade links with this west coast Swedish port. One of the major exports Ellerman's Wilson Line vessels carried to Sweden was British motor vehicle components, which were used in the production of "Volvo" cars and commercial vehicles.*

*The mv. **Salerno** at anchor in Valetta harbour, Malta G.C. This important island was for many years the hub of the Mediterranean trade. It was a very popular run ashore for passenger and crew especially for those of vessels engaged in the North Africa trade.*

AMERICA.

S.S.	Tons.	S.S.	Tons.	S.S.	Tons.
APOLLO	3163	GALILEO	3060	OTHELLO	2479
BUFFALO	4431	HINDOO	3592	OTRANTO	2379
CHICAGO	2729	KOLPINO	2307	RIALTO	2229
COLORADO	4220	LEPANTO	2270	SORRENTO	2208
EBRO	2413	MARENGO	2273	VOLTURNO	2336
FRANCISCO	4582	MARTELLO	3709	PERSIAN MONARCH	3923

S.S. EGYPTIAN MONARCH... 3916   S.S. LYDIAN MONARCH... 3987

From HULL to NEW YORK

(WITH LEAVE TO CALL AT BOSTON).

One of the above full-powered Steamers Weekly.

From NEW YORK to HULL, Weekly.

FROM HULL TO BOSTON, FROM BOSTON TO HULL (with leave to call at NEW YORK), EVERY FORTNIGHT.

These Steamers carry Goods at Through Rates between London, Dundee, Newcastle, Scandinavian, Baltic, &c., and Continental Ports and Western Points United States and Upper Canada, in conjunction with the Steamship Services between Hull and the Ports to which Steamers to and from Hull trade.

The s.s "BUFFALO," and "COLORADO," are splendidly fitted for passengers, with Saloons and sleeping accommodation amidships, and lighted by electricity; and as but a comparatively limited number of passengers are taken, the great size and the speed of these vessels afford much more comfort on the voyage than can be presented by steamers carrying a very large number of passengers. To American Tourists who intend visiting Norway, they give the best opportunity of reaching the starting point for Norway —Hull; and should a few days in England be wished for prior to starting for Norway, Scarborough is but two hours journey and London but five hours from Hull.

LOADING BERTH IN HULL—29 SHED, ALEXANDRA DOCK; IN NEW YORK—BROOKLYN WHARVES.

From LONDON to NEW YORK.

The first-class full-powered passenger Steamers of the WILSON-HILL LINE, Saloons and sleeping accommodation amidships, are intended to sail **Weekly**.

From NEW YORK to LONDON, Weekly.

NEWCASTLE TO NEW YORK. NEW YORK TO NEWCASTLE.

Steamers of the Wilson-Furness Line every Fortnight.

ANTWERP to and from BOSTON and BALTIMORE.---Fortnightly.

ANTWERP to NEW YORK—NEW YORK to ANTWERP, Fortnightly.

HULL to RIVER PLATE PORTS, Steamers to suit the Trade.

Fares.—HULL to NEW YORK, Saloon, Single, £10; Return, £18 (Victualling included).
    ,, LONDON to NEW YORK, Saloon, from £9 9/-, according to accommodation (Victualling included.)
    ,,   ,,   ,, STEERAGE, as cheap as by any other good Line.

AGENTS—SANDERSON & SON, 4, Liberty Square, BOSTON, U.S.
    ,,   SANDERSON & SON, 22, State Street, NEW YORK, U.S.
    ,,   FURNESS, WITHY & CO., LTD., NEWCASTLE-ON-TYNE and BOSTON.
    ,,   PATTERSON, RAMSAY & CO., BALTIMORE.
    ,,   THOS. RONALDSON & CO., ANTWERP, (for Boston and Baltimore Line).
    ,,   D. STEINMANN-HAGHE, ANTWERP, (for New York Line).
    ,,   ALLAN BROS. & CO., 103, Leadenhall Street, LONDON.
    ,,   W. E. BOTT & CO., 1, East India Avenue, Leadenhall Street, LONDON.

For Freight or Passage apply to Thos. Wilson, Sons & Co., Limited, Owners, Hull, or to their Agents (see page 5).

THE BALTIC.

DURING THE SEASON OF OPEN NAVIGATION

Tons.	Tons.	Tons.	Tons.	Tons.
S.S. BRAVO...1074	S.S. GOZO......989	S.S. LEO......1053	S.S. PANTHER 912	S.S. TASSO ...1328
CATO ...1076	HUMBER 596	MILO ...1034	SAPPHO 1113	THURSO 944
FIDO...... 954	KELSO...1054	NERO ...1053	SILVIO ...1193	VOLO ...1289

From HULL to STETTIN every Friday.

Leaving STETTIN for HULL weekly (with leave to call at Copenhagen).

From HULL to DANZIG, From DANZIG to HULL,

EVERY TEN DAYS.

Carrying goods at Through Rates to and from all ports between which the WILSON LINE and steamers to and from Hull trade.   Local traffic carried at cheap rates.

RATES OF PASSAGE :—

	SINGLE.	RETURN.	
1st Class—Hull to Stettin—	£3 3 0	£5 5 0	Victualling—6/6 per day extra.
" " Danzig—	£3 3 0	£5 5 0	" 6/6 " "

LIVERPOOL to DANZIG and STETTIN regularly.

NEWCASTLE TO DANZIG, EVERY 10 DAYS.   NEWCASTLE TO STETTIN, WEEKLY.

AGENTS.

STETTIN, F. IVERS.	DANZIG, F. G. REINHOLD.
LIVERPOOL, R. SANDERSON & CO.	NEWCASTLE, C. HASSELL.

From HULL to COPENHAGEN, Weekly.

Leaving COPENHAGEN for HULL every Thursday.

From LIVERPOOL to COPENHAGEN }
From COPENHAGEN to LIVERPOOL } Regularly during the Season.

The Hull route is particularly recommended to Butter Shippers and Importers.   The Steamers are due to arrive in Hull Sundays, and great attention is paid to prompt despatch of Butter.

RATES OF PASSAGE :—

1st Class—Hull to Copenhagen, Single, £3 3 0; Return, £5 5 0.
Victualling, 6/6 per day extra.

AGENTS—COPENHAGEN, C. K. HANSEN.   LIVERPOOL, R. SANDERSON & CO.

Hull to Malmo and Norrkoping (Steamers to suit the trade)

HULL to STOCKHOLM (Direct) First-class Steamer Weekly during Season.

Passenger accommodation limited.   (The best route for Passengers is *via* Gothenburg.)

These Steamers carry Goods at Through Rates in conjunction with the Steamship Services between Hull and the ports to which Steamers to and from Hull trade.

AGENTS—STOCKHOLM, C. W. BOMAN and J. A. LINDROTH & CO.   MALMO, G. & L. BEIJER.

GRIMSBY TO MALMO, EVERY WEDNESDAY.   MALMO TO GRIMSBY, EVERY THURSDAY.

This route is particularly recommended to Butter Shippers.   The Steamers are due at Grimsby Sundays, and the utmost despatch to forwarding is given.

AGENTS—GRIMSBY, THOS. WILSON, SONS & CO., LIMITED.   MALMO, G. & L. BEIJER.

For Freight or Passage apply to Thos. Wilson, Sons & Co., Limited, Hull, or to their Agents, (see page 5).

THE MEDITERRANEAN AND BLACK SEA.

	TONS.			TONS.			TONS.			TONS
S.S. ALECTO	3607	S.S. CONGO	2906	S.S. MIKADO	3557	S.S. TORO	3067
AUSTRIA	2221	DOURO	2442	MURILLO	2419	TYCHO	3216
CICERO	1834	EBRO	2464	RONDA	1941	URBINO	2429
CLARO	2187	GENOA	1942	SCIPIO	1735	VASCO	1914
CLIO	2733	HINDOO	4980	SAPPHO	1694	VIGO	3252
COLENSO	3861	IAGO	2400	SYRIA	2239	VOLTURNO	2396
		LORENZO	3191	TOKIO	3827		

Hull to Palermo, Messina, Catania, Trieste, Fiume, Venice, and Bari.

Every FORTNIGHT ; leaving the above ports for **HULL** every FORTNIGHT.

Hull to Genoa, Leghorn, Marseilles, and Naples.

About every 14 days ; leaving the above ports for **HULL** about every 14 days.

Hull to Constantinople, Novorossisk and Odessa.

Every 14 days ; leaving **ODESSA** for **HULL** about every 14 days.

Hull to Malta, STEAMERS TO SUIT THE TRADE.

Hull to Alexandria.

Every 14 days ; leaving **ALEXANDRIA FOR HULL** about every 14 days.

London to Trieste, Fiume Venice and Bari.

Every 14 days.

These steamers carry Goods at Cheap Through Rates of Freight to all parts of England, and also in conjunction with the steamship services between Hull and the ports to which steamers to and from Hull trade.

For Freight apply to Thos. Wilson, Sons & Co., Limited, Owners, Hull, or their Agents, see pages 6 and 7

INDIA.

BOMBAY and KURRACHEE, via Suez Canal.

	TONS.			TONS.			TONS.
S.S. ALECTO	3607	S.S. DIDO	4769	S.S. MOROCCO	3783
ALEPPO	3870	LORENZO	3191	OTHELLO	5059
CASTELLO	3635	MIKADO	3557	TOKIO	3827
COLENSO	3861	HINDOO	4980		

HULL TO BOMBAY AND KURRACHEE.   BOMBAY AND KURRACHEE TO HULL.

Fortnightly.   Taking Goods for Port Said.

Middlesbro' to Bombay and Kurrachee.

Fortnightly.   Taking Goods for Port Said.

Some of these Steamers have accommodation amidships for a limited number of Saloon passengers ; they proceed direct to Bombay where passengers disembark. Average passage 30 days. Port Said is the only port usually called at.

Rates of Passage to Bombay : **First Class, £27/10/0 Single ; £50 Return.** Including Victualling.

For Freight or Passage apply to Thos. Wilson, Sons & Co., Limited, Owners, Hull, or to their Agents, see pages 6 and 7.

S.S. ELDORADO.

1382 Tons   2000 Horse Power.

MAIN DECK.

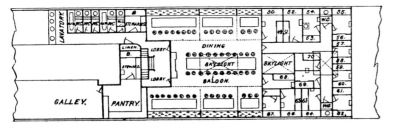

LOWER DECK.

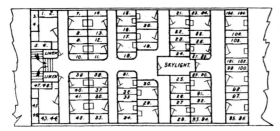

DECK HOUSE.

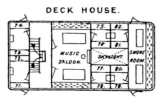

N.B.—ODD NUMBERS ARE UPPER BERTHS.

S.S. ANGELO. 1507 Tons   1300 Horse Power.

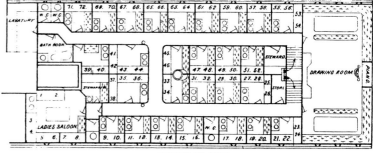

SALOON ON DECK.

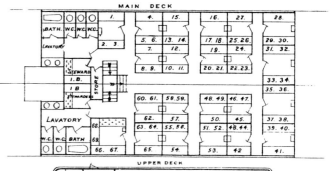

S.S. MONTEBELLO. 1735 Tons   1500 Horse Power.

MAIN DECK

UPPER DECK

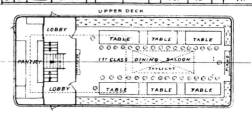

N.B.—ODD NUMBERS ARE UPPER BERTHS.

138

COLORADO (3)	1923	104		ESSEX	1903 (1869)	80
COMO (1)	1871	43				
COMO (2)	1910	88		FAIRY	1903 (1868)	80
CONGO	1890	59		FALCON	1878	50
CONSUELLO (1)	1900	76		FIDO (1)	1867	42
CONSUELLO (2)	1937	105		FIDO (2)	1906	84
CORSO	1894	63		FINLAND	1893 (1884)	62
COURIER	1850	35		FLAMINGO	1878	50
CREST	1839	34		x LEOPARD (1854)		
				FORTO (T)	1939	106
DAGO (1)	1902	77		FRANCISCO (1)	1890	62
DAGO (2)	1947	108		FRANCISCO (2)	1910	89
DARINO	1917	96				
DARLINGTON	1910	88		GALILEO (1)	1881	51
DEFIANCE (T)	1833 (1862)	54		GALILEO (2)	1908	85
DELTA	1903 (1900)	77		GENOA	1903 (1890)	80
DESTRO (1)	1914	93		GITANO (1)	1880	51
DESTRO (2)	1920	97		GITANO (2)	1913	93
DESTRO (3)	1970	113		GITANO (3)	1921	101
DIDO (1)	1862	39		GOURKO	1911	89
DIDO (2)	1896	66		GOZO	1868	42
DIDO (3)	1920	97		GRODNO (1)	1882	54
DOMINO (1)	1877	47		GRODNO (2)	1912	92
DOMINO (2)	1917	96		GRODNO (3)	1919	96
DOMINO (3)	1925	105		GUIDO (1)	1913	93
DOMINO (4)	1947	108		GUIDO (2)	1920	97
DOMINO (5)	1972	113				
DOURO	1889	59		HARROGATE (1)	1911	89
DRACO (1)	1882	54		HARROGATE (2)	1924	105
DRACO (2)	1922	101		HEBE	1861	38
DWINA	1841	34		HERO (1)	1861	38
DYNAMO (1)	1884	55		HERO (2)	1866	42
DYNAMO (2)	1920	97		HERO (3)	1895	63
DYNAMO (3)	1946	107		HERO (4)	1972	113
x KYLEBROOK				HETTY	1894	63
x HOMEWARD (1926)				HIDALGO (1)	1872	46
				HIDALGO (2)	1908	85
EBRO	1889	59		HINDOO (1)	1872	46
ECHO	1863	42		HINDOO (2)	1889	59
ELDORADO (1)	1873	47		HINDOO (3)	1905	84
ELDORADO (2)	1885	55		HORATIO (1)	1893	62
ELDORADO (3)	1886	55		x HORSLEY TOWER		
ELECTRO (1)	1884	55			(1892)	
ELECTRO (2)	1946	107		HORATIO (2)	1896	66
ENVOY	1903 (1872)	80		HULL	1907	85
ERATO (1)	1870	43		HUMBER	1854	35
ERATO (2)	1911	89		HYDRO (1)	1899	76
ERATO (3)	1923	104		HYDRO (2)	1911	89
ESKIMO	1910	89				
ESPERANZA	1903 (1871)	80		IAGO (1)	1889	59

IAGO (2)	1921	101
x SANTE FE (1901)		
IDAHO (1)	1896	66
IDAHO (2)	1898	67
IDAHO (3)	1903	84
INO	1868	42
IRWELL	1854	35
IVANHOE	1837	34
JAFFA	1903 (1897)	80
JUMBO (T)	1888	58
JUNO (1)	1861	38
JUNO (2)	1864	39
JUNO (3)	1869	43
JUNO (4)	1882	54
JUNO (5)	1889	59
JUNO (6)	1900	76
KATIE	1920	100
KELSO (1)	1869	43
KELSO (2)	1909	88
KELSO (3)	1924	104
KINGSTON	1856	35
KOLPINO (1)	1889	59
KOLPINO (2)	1906	84
KOTKA	1903 (1895)	80
KOVNO (1)	1882	54
KOVNO (2)	1907	85
KYNO (1)	1913	93
KYNO (2)	1924	104
LEO (1)	1869	43
LEO (2)	1920	100
x SPES (1908)		
LEO (3)	1947	108
LEOPARD	1878 (1854)	50
LEPANTO (1)	1877	50
LEPANTO (2)	1915	96
LIDO	1901	77
LIVORNO (1)	1878	50
x MARSDIN (1870)		
LIVORNO (2)	1909	88
LIVORNO (3)	1946	107
LORENZO	1893	62
x LANSDOWNE TOWER (1890)		
LORNE	1903 (1873)	80
LUMSDEN	1878	50
MALMO (1)	1888	38
x PACIFIC (1860)		

MALMO (2)	1946	107
MANCHURIAN	1920	100
x TILLY RUSS (1905)		
MARENGO (1)	1879	51
MARENGO (2)	1910	89
MARENGO (3)	1947	108
MARSDIN	1878 (1870)	50
MARTELLO	1884	55
MIKARDO	1894	63
MILO	1865	39
MONTEBELLO (1)	1890	62
MONTEBELLO (2)	1911	92
MOROCCO	1900	76
MOSQUITO	1884	55
MOURINO (1)	1877	50
MOURINO (2)	1906	85
MURILLO	1893	63
NARVA	1903 (1883)	80
NAVARINO	1873	47
NERO (1)	1868	43
NERO (2)	1909	88
NERO (3)	1924	104
x CLADDAGH		
x TRUTHFUL		
x SUSSEX COAST (1907)		
NEVA	1856	35
NORTH EASTERN	1861	38
NORTH SEA	1855	35
NOVO	1902	77
ODER	1861	39
OHIO	1887	58
x EGYPTIAN MONARCH (1881)		
ONTARIO	1887	58
x LYDIAN MONARCH (1881)		
ORIA	1903 (1880)	80
ORLANDO (1)	1869	43
ORLANDO (2)	1920	100
x INANDA (1904)		
OSCAR	1847	34
OSLO	1906	85
OSWEGO	1916	96
OSWY	1831	34
OTHELLO (1)	1872	47
OTHELLO (2)	1897	66
OTRANTO	1877	50
OTTO (1)	1867	42
OTTO (2)	1898	67

Name	Year	No.
OUSE	1862	39
OXFORD	1903 (1870)	81
PACIFIC	1860	38
PALERMO (1)	1872	47
PALERMO (2)	1938	105
PANTHER	1878	50
PATRIOT	1840	34
PERA	1903 (1899)	81
PERSIAN MONARCH	1887 (1880)	58
PETER & JANE	1831	34
PLATO (1)	1868	43
PLATO (2)	1878	50
x TIGER (1857)		
PLATO (3) (T)	1901	77
POLO (1)	1889	59
POLO (2)	1913	93
POLO (3)	1919	96
PRESTO (1) (T)	1894	63
x TRIUMPH (1893)		
PRESTO (2) (T)	1946	107
xEMPIRE SARA (1943)		
QUITO	1870	43
RAPALLO	1960	109
RIALTO (1)	1878	51
RIALTO (2)	1949	109
RINALDO (1)	1872	47
RINALDO (2)	1908	85
RINALDO (3)	1946	107
ROLLO (1)	1870	43
ROLLO (2)	1920	100
x ITALIAN		
x FANTEE (1899)		
ROLLO (3)	1954	109
ROMANO	1880	54
ROMEO	1881	54
RONDA	1903 (1898)	81
ROSARIO	1883	54
RUNO (1)	1902	77
RUNO (2)	1920	97
SACREMENTO	1945	106
SALERNO (1)	1879	51
SALERNO (2)	1889	55
x CHICAGO		
x LINCOLN CITY (1884)		
SALERNO (3)	1912	92
SALERNO (4)	1924	104
SALERNO (5)	1965	112
SALMO (1)	1900	76
SALMO (2)	1924	105
SALMO (3)	1967	112
SALVO (T)	1898	76
SAMBO (T)	1896	47
x ZERO (1) (1876)		
SANGRO	1968	112
SANTIAGO	1886	55
SAPPHO (1)	1864	39
SAPPHO (2)	1898	67
SAPPHO (3)	1903	84
SCANDINAVIAN	1852	35
SCIPIO	1895	63
SELBY	1922	101
SERBINO	1912	92
SERGEI	1920	67
x CASTRO (1899)		
SILVIO (1)	1880	51
SILVIO (2)	1913	93
SILVIO (3)	1947	108
SILVIO (4)	1968	112
SMOLENSK	1916	96
SORRENTO (1)	1878	51
SORRENTO (2)	1912	92
SORRENTO (3)	1967	112
SPERO (1)	1896	66
SPERO (2)	1922	101
SPERO (3)	1966	112
SULTAN	1903 (1867)	81
SULTANA	1903 (1888)	81
SUSAN	1850	34
SWALLOW	1866	42
SWIFT	1831	34
SYRIA	1903 (1889)	81
TASSO (1)	1870	35
x SCANDINAVIAN (1852)		
TASSO (2)	1890	62
TASSO (3)	1922	104
TASSO (4)	1938	105
TASSO (5)	1945	106
TEANO (1)	1913	93
TEANO (2)	1925	105
TEANO (3)	1955	109
THOMAS RICKENSON	1839	34
THOMAS WILSON	1870	43
THURSO (1)	1885	55
x EASTELLA (1871)		
THURSO (2)	1909	88

THURSO (3)	1919	97
x WAR BRAMBLE (1919)		
TIGER	1878 (1857)	50
TINTO (1)	1911	92
TINTO (2)	1947	108
TOKIO	1895	63
TOLEDO	1881	54
TORCELLO (1)	1912	92
TORCELLO (2)	1920	100
x STAHLOF (1911)		
TORO	1904	84
TORONTO	1900	76
TORPEDO	1885	55
TOSNO	1907	85
TRENT	1862	39
TRENTINO (1)	1919	97
TRENTINO (2)	1952	109
TRURO (1)	1898	67
TRURO (2)	1922	104
TRURO (3)	1947	108
TYCHO	1904	84
UNA	1903 (1899)	81
UNITED SERVICE	1862	39
URBINO (1)	1871	46
URBINO (2)	1889	59
URBINO (3)	1915	96
URBINO (4)	1919	97
VARRO (T)	1912	92
VASCO (1)	1895	63
VASCO (2)	1920	101
x BRANDENBURG (1910)		
VASCO (3)	1939	106
VIGO	1905	84
VIRAGO	1871	46
VOLO (1)	1890	62
VOLO (2)	1938	105
VOLO (3)	1946	107
VOLTURNO	1888	58
WALAMO	1871	46
WAVE	1848	34
WILLIAM BAILEY	1903 (1883)	81
XANTHO	1871	46
YEDDO	1871	46
YORK	1907	85
ZAIMIS	1898	67
ZARA	1903 (1897)	81
ZEBRA	1878	51
ZENO	1871	46
ZERO (1) (T)	1976	47
ZERO (2)	1896	66